THE
SEVEN SECRETS
OF SUCCESSFUL
COACHES

How to Unlock and Unleash
Your Team's Full Potential

Jeff Janssen & Greg Dale

Winning The Mental Game
Cary, North Carolina

This publication is designed to provide accurate and authoritative information in regard to the subject matter covered. It is sold with the understanding that the publisher is not engaged in rendering legal, accounting, or other professional services. If legal advice or other expert assistance is required, the services of a competent professional person should be sought.

Every effort has been made to trace the ownership of all quotations used in this book. In the event of a question arising about a quotation, we regret any error made and will be pleased to make the necessary correction in future editions of this book.

Substantial discounts on bulk quantities of this book are available to corporations, professional associations, and other organizations. For details and discount information, please contact the publisher.

Published by Winning The Mental Game
102 Horne Creek Court, Cary, NC 27519
Phone: 1-888-721-TEAM
Website: www.jeffjanssen.com

Publisher's Cataloging-in-Publication
(Provided by Quality Books, Inc.)

Janssen, Jeff.
   The seven secrets of successful coaches : how to
unlock and unleash your team's full potential / Jeff
Janssen & Greg Dale.
   p. cm.
Includes bibliographical references and index.
LCCN: 2001096194
ISBN: 1-892882-02-7

   1. Coaching (Athletics) 2. Teamwork (Sports)
3. Leadership.   I. Dale, Greg. II. Title.

GV711.J36.2002   796.07'7
                       QBI0I-201256

Printed in the United States of America

10 9 8 7 6 5 4

DEDICATION

To the three most credible coaches in my life...

My mom, Mary—thanks for investing so much or yourself in me.

My dad, Tom—thanks for being the President of my Fan Club.

My wife, Kristi—thanks for being my best friend—we make a great team!

I hope that I can be as credible of a "coach" to Ryan and Jill
as you have been to me!

Jeff Janssen

To my wife, Cammie—you are my best friend
and the best mother three children could possibly have. Thanks for
everything you do to make our family a great team!

To my mom, Dolores—thanks for always being there for me.

To my dad, Shep—thanks for being a great coach during my life—
keep your chin up and finish strong.

To my two brothers, Mike and Chris—know that I think
about you both every day.

Greg Dale

TABLE OF CONTENTS

ACKNOWLEDGMENTS

Just as good leaders look to distribute the credit, we too would like to express our sincere appreciation to all of the people who assisted us with this book.

First, thank you to the many credible coaches who shared their time and insights with us: Mike Candrea, Gail Goestenkors, Tom Renney, Terry Pettit, Mary Wise, Leroy Walker, Fred Harvey, Jerry Welsh, Jeff Meyer, Pat Summitt, Mike Krzyzewski, Roy Williams, Jerry Yeagley, Gary Barnett, Marty Schottenheimer, Rhonda Revelle, Josh Pastner, Mike Pressler, Jolene Nagel, Mike Gillespie, and Kerstin Kimel. We appreciate your willingness to share the ideas that make you such special people.

Thank you to the people who provided us with their comments and suggestions on drafts of the book including: Rhonda Revelle, Bart Lerner, Bob Harmison, Joe Whitney, Shelley Wiechman, Kimberley Amirault, Mary Wise, Terry Pettit, Greg Allen, Cathy Klein, David Hartman, Keith Henschen, Rich Gordin, Dan Kenney, Jeff Meyer, Scott Martin, and in particular, Jamie Robbins and Jill McCartney. Your great ideas took this book to another level that we couldn't have reached without your help.

Thank you to Cathy Schmitt, Donna Bazzell, Cynthia Prieto, and Debbie Williamson for the countless hours you spent transcribing the interview tapes. We really appreciate your help. A special thank you to Judy Byron for your graphic design work and expertise as well as the great people at Data Reproductions.

Jeff would like to thank the following:

A very sincere thank you to all of the credible coaches who I have been privileged to interact with through the years—from the ones who coached me, to the ones who have attended my programs, to the ones who have trusted me to work with their teams. Please know how much I respect what you are doing—continue being coaches of significance.

Thank you to my parents, Tom and Mary Janssen. Dad, although we can't see your smile anymore, know that you have left a lasting legacy with Jaclyn and me about how special and precious families are. Mom, thanks for investing so much of yourself in me. Through your words and example you have truly taught me what it means to be a credible and loving leader. Thanks for being the best role model.

Finally, thanks to my special family for allowing me the time to pursue one of my passions to co-author this book. Kristi, you are my best friend and I truly appreciate your support, companionship, and love. And to my children, Ryan and Jill, I adore both of you. Your job is to make sure that I practice what I preach in this book. I hope that you are proud of the way I live my dash.

Greg would like to thank the following:

I have had the opportunity to play for, coach along side, and consult with some of the most highly credible coaches in the world. I want all of you to know how much I appreciate your guidance and trust in me. I know I am a much better person as a result of spending time with all of you.

Thanks to Shep and Dolores—my parents. Dad, you have shown me the importance of having a sense of humor and a pursuit of excellence. Mom, you have always been my inspiration. I admire your drive and determination as well as your tender heart.

Last but certainly not least, I would like to thank Cammie, Abbey, Graham, and Jacob for allowing me to pursue the goal of writing this book. Cammie, you have been so supportive when I needed to spend extra time in the office. Abbey, Graham, and Jacob, you bring me immeasurable joy. I hope the three of you maintain your incredible zest for life and always help me to remember the important things in life.

INTRODUCTION

Have you ever wondered why some coaches achieve so much success with their athletes and teams—winning championships and everyone's respect along the way—while others continually fall short or struggle to get their teams to play over .500? If you are like most coaches, you have probably found yourself both fascinated and frustrated by the following questions:

- How do some coaches build and maintain championship level programs year after year even though everyone else is trying desperately to knock them off?

- How do some coaches come in and resurrect losing programs with a long and demoralizing history of defeat and quickly guide them to a championship level?

- How do some coaches consistently get the most out of their athletes while others have athletes who chronically underachieve?

- How do some coaches gain their athletes' confidence, trust, and respect while others have athletes who never buy into them and what they are trying to accomplish?

- How do some coaches inspire their athletes to play with confidence, aggressiveness, and mental toughness while others have athletes who routinely crumble and choke under pressure?

- How do some coaches get their athletes to willingly "run through walls" for them while others have athletes with little commitment, no work ethic, and bad attitudes?

- How do some coaches inspire a sense of loyalty and pride in their athletes while others have athletes who look to transfer or, worse yet, instigate a revolt and try to get their coaches fired?

It All Starts At the Top

The purpose of this book is to provide you with the answers to these intriguing and important leadership questions. After all, these answers are the core of what successful coaching is all about—getting athletes and teams to consistently perform to their full potential. The world's most successful coaches have the special ability to bring out the absolute best in the people they lead.

You have probably heard the saying "It all starts at the top." This saying could not be more true when it comes to the kind of impact that you have on your team's success. Your leadership is the key component in deciding whether your team will perform to its potential or fall short of it.

Don't get us wrong. Certainly your athletes are a huge part of the success equation. They are the ones who actually play the game and deserve much of the credit when your team does well. Yet without your ability to attract, motivate, develop, discipline, produce, and keep good athletes, your team has little chance of being successful on a consistent basis. As a coach, you are the one who sets the tone for your team and the person who is ultimately responsible for creating a winning environment for your athletes.

"If the coach is organized, everything falls into place. If he has self-discipline, then the team has discipline. If he's dedicated, the team is dedicated. Everything revolves around the head coach. He's the one who has to make the team go."
Ray Nitschke, Former Green Bay Packer Coached by Vince Lombardi

"An institution is the lengthened shadow of one man."
Ralph Waldo Emerson

So if you aspire to be a more successful coach—one who is able to build and maintain a winning program, one who is able to inspire and develop athletes to reach their potential, one who earns his or her athletes' trust, loyalty, and respect, and one who creates winners both on and off the court or field, then this book was written specifically for you.

Why Not Learn from the Best?

Because coaches play such a critical role in creating and maintaining a team's success, we interviewed many of sport's most respected and successful coaches to discover their secrets for developing championship athletes and teams. As Peak Performance Consultants who have worked with some of the nation's top universities, we have had the awesome privilege to work with, observe, and interview many of sport's top coaches including:

Mike Candrea, Head Softball Coach, University of Arizona

A three-time National Coach of the Year, Mike Candrea has led Arizona Softball to six national championships. Candrea is also the head coach of the United States national team and guided USA Softball to win the gold medal in Athens in 2004.

Mike Gillespie, Head Baseball Coach, University of Southern California

Since taking over the helm at USC, Coach Gillespie has led the Trojans to four Pacific-10 Southern Division titles and one National Championship. He has been named National Coach of the Year once, the Pac-10 Coach of the Year three times, and the West Region Coach of the Year twice.

Gail Goestenkors, Head Women's Basketball Coach, Duke University

Coach Goestenkors has guided the Blue Devils to three Final Fours and an appearance in the national championship game. Her Duke teams have won five consecutive Atlantic Coast Conference regular season titles and she has been named ACC Coach of the Year six times. In 2004, she also served as an assistant coach with USA Basketball helping the U.S. win the gold medal in Athens.

Fred Harvey, Head Track and Field Coach, University of Arizona

As one of the nation's top sprints coaches, Fred Harvey has developed numerous national champions, All-Americans, and Olympians.

Mike Krzyzewski, Head Men's Basketball Coach, Duke University

With three national championships, three National Coach of the Year awards, and an induction into the basketball Hall of Fame, Mike Krzyzewski is considered one of college basketball's premiere coaches. He also served as an assistant coach with the Olympic Dream Team in 1992.

Terry Pettit, Former Head Volleyball Coach, University of Nebraska

Coach Pettit built Nebraska into one of the nation's best programs leading the Huskers to six Final Fours and one national championship. Coach Pettit presently serves in a unique position as the Coach Advocate for the University of Nebraska coaching staff.

Tom Renney, Director of Player Personnel, New York Rangers

Tom Renney led the Canadian national hockey team to a silver medal finish in the Lillehammer Olympics in 1994. He also coached the NHL's Vancouver Canucks. Presently Tom serves as the Director of Player Personnel for the New York Rangers.

Rhonda Revelle, Head Softball Coach, University of Nebraska

As Nebraska softball's all-time winningest coach, Rhonda Revelle led the Huskers to a Big 12 conference championship and one Women's College World Series appearance. She is also the president of the National Fastpitch Coaches Association.

Marty Schottenheimer, Head Football Coach, San Diego Chargers

After leading the Kansas City Chiefs to three AFC Central titles and the NFL's second highest win percentage in the 1990's, Marty Schottenheimer is the head coach of the San Diego Chargers.

Pat Summitt, Head Women's Basketball Coach, University of Tennessee

Not only has Coach Summitt led the Lady Vols to six national championships including a rare three-peat in 1996-98, she has been inducted into both the Naismith Basketball Hall of Fame and the Women's Basketball Hall of Fame.

Leroy Walker, Former North Carolina Central Track Coach

Dr. Walker is the former president of the United States Olympic Committee. He has coached 77 All-Americans, 40 national champions, and eight Olympians. He was the head men's coach for the U.S. Olympic Track and Field Team in Montreal in 1976. Dr. Walker has been inducted into the U.S. Olympic Hall of Fame.

Jerry Welsh, Scout, Milwaukee Bucks

Coach Welsh had successful tenures as basketball coach at Potsdam University and Iona College. His teams at Potsdam won two national championships and he was named NCAA Division III Basketball Coach of the Year four times during his career.

Roy Williams, Head Men's Basketball Coach, University of North Carolina

In 2003, Roy Williams returned to his alma mater to coach the University of North Carolina men's basketball program. Previously at the University of Kansas, Coach Williams won more games in the first 12 seasons of his career than anyone else in NCAA history, including three Final Fours.

Mary Wise, Head Volleyball Coach, University of Florida

A two-time National Coach of the Year honoree, Coach Wise has led the Gators to an unprecedented 12 SEC conference championships and six Final Four appearances.

Jerry Yeagley, Head Men's Soccer Coach, Indiana University

One of soccer's legendary coaches, Coach Yeagley has coached the Hoosiers to six national championships. A five-time National Coach of the Year, Coach Yeagley retired after the 2003 season as the all-time winningest coach in men's soccer history.

Through our interactions and interviews with these championship coaches, you will get a behind-the-scenes look at the seldom-shared strategies they use to get the most out of their athletes and teams. Additionally, we will share stories, insights, and quotes with you from many other highly successful coaches including Joe Torre, Dean Smith, Tommy Lasorda, John Wooden, Tom Osborne, Phil Jackson, Amos Alonzo Stagg, Anson Dorrance, Dan Gable, Vince Lombardi, Rick Pitino, and Bill Walsh. By examining the combined wisdom of so many of sport's top coaches, you too will learn how to unlock and unleash your athletes' full potential.

"You must study the people who have been successful as leaders. Whether you call it modeling or using a mentor or simply following people in your profession you admire, the method is the same. You have to learn from the people who are successful. You especially have to recognize the traits that enabled them to be successful."

Rick Pitino, University of Louisville Men's Basketball

Discover What Athletes Want and Need From You for Peak Performance

In addition to interviewing and studying dozens of highly successful coaches, we spoke to hundreds of athletes from almost every sport and level to discover their insights on what it takes to be a successful coach. Thus, you will hear directly from many athletes about specific strategies you can use to help them consistently perform to their potential. And, on the flip side, you will also hear athletes tell you in their own words the things you absolutely must avoid doing.

Coaches, CEOs, Managers, Teachers, and Parents Can All Benefit from this Book

In essence, this book is about how you can get the most out of your people by being an effective leader. Although we use successful sport coaches as our exemplars, the powerful and proven leadership principles presented in this book apply to leaders from all walks of life. Whether you are a CEO, manager, teacher, or parent, you will gain numerous insights and ideas to help you become a more effective and credible leader.

Those in the business world can simply substitute the word "manager" for coach and "employee" for athlete. Many businesses already use the concept of "coaching" to get the most out of their people. In fact, Federal Express and several other Fortune 500 companies use the principles in this book to gain an essential edge in the competitive corporate arena.

Similarly, teachers can also adapt these leadership principles to the classroom setting to earn the respect of their students and take them to new levels of achievement and personal growth. Additionally, parents can use these principles to develop powerful and loving relationships with their children based on mutual respect and trust.

"I still think the most important aspects of coaching are credibility, trust, and communication. If you have those things going for you in football, you'll win. And if you have them going for you as a business executive, you will win, too. They are the fundamental building blocks to success in any field."

Marty Schottenheimer, San Diego Chargers

Let's Begin Our Journey

So no matter what kind of leader you are or what type of team you lead, if you aspire to be the kind of coach who helps people develop to their full potential, then this book is definitely for you. Throughout the book, you will learn proven strategies that will help you create more confident, committed, and coachable athletes. In Chapter 1 you'll discover how highly successful coaches define success. In Chapter 2 you will learn how to earn your athletes' and colleagues' respect by being a credible coach. In Chapter 3 you will learn the benefits of being a credible coach and why it is the absolute key for getting the most out of your athletes. In Chapter 4 you will discover the seven secrets that successful coaches have in common. Chapter 5 covers a variety of developmental stages in which you might find yourself as your coaching philosophy evolves over time. Chapter 6 provides you with a step-by-step process for assessing and improving your credibility. Chapters 7-13 take an in depth look at each of the seven secrets of successful coaches, giving you a wealth of practical tips for building your credibility as well as sustaining it over the long term. Plus, at the end of many chapters, we will feature ten of sport's best coaches as they share their wisdom on what it takes to be a successful coach.

We look forward to accompanying you on your journey to getting the absolute most out of the people you lead. We truly believe that this book will have a tremendous impact on your overall success and satisfaction as a coach/leader, which in turn will positively affect the success and satisfaction of the people you lead. Thanks for letting us join you on your journey!

Kerstin Kimel, Head Women's Lacrosse Coach, Duke University

CHAPTER ONE

WHAT IT TAKES TO BE A SUCCESSFUL COACH

"Everybody has the X's and O's. It's your ability to be organized and to communicate with people. That is what differentiates the successful coaches."
Mary Wise, University of Florida Volleyball

What does it take to be a successful coach? This is one of the first questions we asked in our interviews with highly successful coaches. As you begin this book, we challenge you to think about your response to the same question.

Success is Much More Than X's and O's

Interestingly, while coaches flock to clinics to listen to the championship coaches we feature in this book and frantically scribble down the X's and O's of their offenses, defenses, schemes, and systems, the coaches we interviewed admit that their true secrets of success lie elsewhere. They believe that the X's and O's are certainly important, however, they insist that their success depends more on how they relate to and motivate their athletes.

"Coaches who can outline plays on a blackboard are a dime a dozen. The ones who win get inside their players' heads and motivate."
Vince Lombardi, Former Green Bay Packers Coach

"There are no secrets with the X's and O's. We all know that. I think the coaches who are successful find a way to get the best out of each individual on their team; to help them reach their potential. That's the real challenge."

Jerry Yeagley, Indiana University Men's Soccer

"There is very little difference in technical knowledge about the game of basketball among most experienced coaches. However, there is a vast difference between leaders in their ability to teach and motivate those under their supervision. You must have the more elusive ability to teach and to motivate. This defines a leader; if you can't teach and you can't motivate, you can't lead."

John Wooden, Former UCLA Men's Basketball Coach

The Coach's Funeral

In addition to attributing their success to factors that went way beyond the X's and O's, the successful coaches we interviewed also defined success in a very unique way. We believe the following story might help you better understand their definition of success.

Some years ago a local high school coach passed away after a long and illustrious career. His teams had won twelve conference championships, three state championships, and he retired as the state's all-time winningest coach. Upon hearing the news of his death, the vast majority of his former players, both young and old, came from near and far to attend their coach's funeral. So many of the coach's past players were there that a line stretched half way around the funeral parlor.

A local townswoman, noticing the long line of former players, turned to one of them and said, "Wow, your coach must have really been a special person. Just look at all of the guys who have come from all over to pay their last respects. This really must be a sad and terrible day. I feel so sorry for you all."

The man turned to the woman and said rather sheepishly, "Actually ma'am, even though Coach might have won a lot of games, he was one of the biggest jerks most of us have ever known. He screamed at us, humiliated us, and tortured the heck out of us. The real reason we all came back to town is to make sure that sucker is really dead!"

Unfortunately, there are still some coaches who use wins as their only measure of success, regardless of how they come by them. Some coaches have outstanding winning percentages but do so in ways that demean, embarrass, and intimidate athletes. Sadly, their athletes actually despise them and feel that they win in spite of their coaches, not because of them. When this is the case, we feel that victories are somewhat tarnished and hollow if the coaches are not also respected by their athletes. While they might be successful on the court or field, we believe these coaches have actually lost in the long run and should not be looked to as models for other aspiring leaders to follow.

"I know that you can have success being an autocrat and not relating to your players. But you know what, that isn't the kind of success that I want to have. The satisfaction of success cannot be measured by wins and losses. It is about making a difference and helping people achieve their goals within a team situation."

Marty Schottenheimer, San Diego Chargers

True Success is More Than Wins

As you consider your definition of success, remember that ultimately your success as a coach will not solely be judged on the quantity of wins you have, but also on the quality of the relationships you develop with your athletes. Even if some day you are fortunate to amass enough wins to be inducted into your sport's Hall of Fame, consider if it is truly worth it to you if few of your athletes would be happy for you or want to attend the induction ceremony.

Despite winning numerous Coach of the Year honors, and conference and national championships, the successful coaches we interviewed did not use winning as their only, nor most important measure of success. Instead, we found that many of sport's most successful and respected coaches had a much broader and deeper definition of success.

"Your definition of success should have more depth than the equivalent of winning a national championship."

Mike Krzyzewski, Duke University Men's Basketball

"Rings don't mean that you are a champion. It's that kid 10 years from now who calls you up and says, 'You know what? You were very special in my life.' That's what it's all about."

Mike Candrea, University of Arizona Softball

"If I can help an individual reach his potential, then I think regardless of the record, I have been successful. Some of my best and most successful teams have not been national championship teams."

Jerry Yeagley, Indiana University Men's Soccer

As you can see from the previous quotes, the coaches we interviewed believe that winning games and championships is simply not enough. To be considered truly successful they must also help their athletes develop to their full potential, on and off the court or field. Successful coaches not only teach their players sport skills, they also teach them life skills.

Our interviews with athletes confirmed that successful coaches do much more than win games—they also win their athletes' respect. Many of the athletes we interviewed were eager to share what a profound impact their coaches had made on their lives—both as an athlete and as a person. We continually heard comments like:

"Coach brought out the best in me."
"I have the utmost respect for Coach."
"Coach is like a second mom or dad to me."
"Coach just makes you want to be good."
"I would run through a wall for Coach."

Thus the definition of success we will use for this book is the same one espoused by the highly successful coaches we interviewed. True success means winning in ways that cause your athletes to respect you for it. In fact, as you will see in the next chapter and throughout the rest of the book, the primary reason why successful coaches win is because they have earned their athletes' respect and trust.

Questions for Reflection

- What does it take to be a successful coach?
- Do you define success only in terms of wins and losses?
- Have you won the respect of your athletes?

Chapter One Key Points

- Remember that being a successful coach is much more than the X's and O's of coaching.
- To be truly successful, you must not only win games but also the respect of your athletes.

Fred Harvey, Head Track Coach, University of Arizona

CHAPTER TWO

HOW TO WIN RESPECT BY BEING A CREDIBLE COACH

"My ideas about how to command respect have changed... I've learned that you can't demand it, or whack it out of people with a two-by-four. You have to cultivate it, in yourself and those around you."

Pat Summitt, University of Tennessee Women's Basketball

As we discussed in the opening chapter, true success as a coach means that you not only win games and championships, but it also means that you win the respect of your athletes. In addition to helping you attain a meaningful and lasting sense of success and satisfaction, winning your athletes' respect is also the best way to help them reach their full potential.

Coercive Coaches Attempt to Force Respect

"I really do much better under a coach who doesn't feel like he or she has to embarrass me in front of others to motivate me. I have had coaches who use that as a tactic and others that don't. Those coaches that don't, get so much more out of me."

College Women's Lacrosse Player

How do you earn your athletes' respect? Not too long ago, most coaches believed that the best way to gain respect was to be a stern, unemotional, and unrelenting disciplinarian who ordered people around like a traditional military drill sergeant. These coaches believed that respect must be demanded from their athletes. So they told people what to do and used threats and intimidation to get them to do it. They believed that the tougher they were on their athletes, the more they would respect them. This "command and control" style of leadership we have come to call coercive coaching. We use the term "coercive" mainly because athletes follow these coaches not because they want to, but more because they have to so that they can avoid their coaches' wrath.

The problem with the coercive approach is that true respect must be earned from people, not imposed on them. Coercive coaches force people to follow them out of fear. They make athletes fear them by punishing, embarrassing, and yelling at them when they make mistakes or break rules. While their athletes do often comply with their commands, coercive coaches are not legitimate leaders. They function more like dictators, intimidators, and masters of manipulation who might be obeyed, but are not respected. This overbearing and negative approach may work in the short term, but over the long run it leads to people who feel discouraged, persecuted, humiliated, and incompetent. It is not surprising that athletes soon come to resist and resent coercive coaches.

"I didn't want to be a dictator to my players or assistant coaches or managers. For me, concern, compassion, and consideration were always priorities of the highest order."

John Wooden, Former UCLA Men's Basketball Coach

"It's sad to me when you see 40 and 50 year old coaches using fear and intimidation to try to motivate teenage kids who are less than half of their age."

Mike Candrea, University of Arizona Softball

"Appreciate the fact that you cannot lead without eager followers."

Pat Summitt, University of Tennessee Women's Basketball

To get a better picture of the coercive approach, imagine the following scenario: After a tough, close loss to your rival team, your athletic director strangely appears in your locker room with a crazed look in his eyes. In front of your entire team he begins screaming at you at the top of his lungs,

"You are such a terrible coach! I can't believe some of the stupid decisions you made down the stretch. You lost the game for us. If you don't win next week, I'll fire you and we'll get someone in here who can actually coach!" He then storms out leaving both you and your athletes stunned. How would you feel and respond after such a tirade?

Fortunately, extremely few athletic directors would be unprofessional enough to do such a thing. The hypothetical scenario is totally inappropriate and would likely have a disastrous effect on all involved. If this coercive approach is so appalling for an athletic director to use with a coach, why then do so many coaches still use the coercive approach with their athletes?

Perhaps the coercive coaching style was somewhat effective years ago primarily because athletes automatically respected their coach's authority. If a coach said "Jump," the athletes jumped, no questions asked. Some coaches thrived in this era because of their tough, domineering, hard-nosed approach.

However, just as society continually evolves and changes, so too has the kind of coaching to which athletes respond best. The coercive coaching style, which once seemed to work, has given way to a more effective style. This approach, which we call credible coaching, has evolved because people no longer respect leaders just because of their position or title, but now believe that leaders must earn their respect.

"I was a major league ballplayer for sixteen years, and some of my managers were old-school characters who used fear and threats to try to motivate. You can't do that anymore."

Joe Torre, New York Yankees

"The traditional coaching style is often that of a drill sergeant who motivates through intimidation and fear. As the years went by, I became more convinced that love was stronger than any source of motivation, even fear."

Tom Osborne, Former University of Nebraska Football Coach

"The most essential thing for a leader to have is the respect of those under his or her supervision. It starts with giving them respect."

John Wooden, Former UCLA Basketball Coach

Credible Coaches Earn Respect

Credible coaches earn their athletes' respect by the way they nurture and develop them. First and foremost, they treat their athletes with dignity and respect and basically abide by the Golden Rule—they treat people the way they would like to be treated. Credible coaches are honest and trustworthy in their dealings with their athletes. They are not afraid to show their athletes how much they care about them—both as athletes and people. Because credible coaches are genuine and inspiring in their approach, they create an environment where athletes feel valued, appreciated, challenged, and competent. In doing so they build their athletes' confidence and guide them to their goals. In general, credible coaches build solid relationships with their athletes based on integrity, compassion, and trust.

"Never underestimate the value of compassion, honesty, and trust in dealing with your athletes."

Tom Renney, Director of Player Personnel, New York Rangers

Our interviews and experiences with successful coaches and their athletes confirm that credible coaching is the best way to help your athletes develop to their full potential. If you want your athletes to give you their absolute best, they need to respect and trust you. Athletes consciously or subconsciously ask themselves "Can I trust you? Do you know what you are talking about? Are you committed to excellence? Do you care about me?" Only when your athletes believe you are a credible coach, will they wholeheartedly follow you. They will give you the most important ingredient you need to be truly successful—their hearts. Credible coaches know that people will give them their best if they treat them well and create an environment that is conducive to high performance. And in turn, their athletes respect them.

"Leadership isn't really about leading people. It's about getting them to follow you."

Steve Young, Former San Francisco 49ers Quarterback

"I think it is extremely important to have the respect of the players."

Dean Smith, Former University of North Carolina Men's Basketball Coach

"If you don't have your athletes' respect, they're never going to trust you or do what you want them to do."

Fred Harvey, Head Track Coach, University of Arizona

Earning Respect is Not the Same as Getting Athletes to Like You

Earning your athletes' respect does not mean that you are trying to get them to like you. Getting everyone to like you and the decisions you make is virtually an impossible task. Starting positions and playing time must be determined which obviously will please some athletes and upset others. Since you can't please everyone all of the time, you must focus on making decisions that will be the best for the team. In doing so, you will earn the respect of your team. And when you are respected, you will very likely be liked as well. Thus, the key principle to keep in mind is this: If you focus on being liked, you will probably not be respected. However, if you focus on earning your athletes' respect, you will probably be liked as well.

"It's important for the coach to be respected. Personally I wouldn't want to coach if most or, in fact all of the players didn't like me also. But I would never compensate any type of decision, or be less in my decision making, in trying to pursue the 'like' part of it. I would really go after the respect. But I would like to be admired, liked, and respected by my players."

Mike Krzyzewski, Duke University Men's Basketball

"If your players respect you, you can have a very good working environment. If they respect you and like you, you can have a very harmonious working environment. If they dislike you and don't respect you, then it's just poison—it's your death. So if you can only pick one, you choose respect."

Rhonda Revelle, University of Nebraska Softball

"It's interesting to me because you hear coaches say all the time, 'I don't want to be liked, I just want to be respected.' Believe me, if players like you and respect you, they'll do just about anything for you."

Marcus Allen, Former Kansas City Chiefs Football Player

Contrasting Coercive Coaches and Credible Coaches

The chart below contrasts the approaches taken by coercive and credible coaches. Think about some of the past coaches you played for. Which approach did they tend to use the most? Then think about yourself. Which approach do you use the most?

Coercive Coaches...	Credible Coaches...
seek to rule and control	*seek to relate and connect*
command	*communicate*
manipulate with fear	*motivate with future goals*
intimidate and embarrass	*inspire and empower*
ridicule for failure	*reward for success*
are sarcastic and critical	*are sensitive and complimentary*
criticize and torture	*challenge and teach*
focus on problems and obstacles	*focus on potential and opportunities*
are obstinate and aloof	*are open-minded and approachable*
demand all the credit	*distribute all the credit*
create compliant and tentative athletes	*create compelled and trusting athletes*
create team conflict	*create team chemistry*
are resisted and resented	*are respected and revered*

Ironically, coaches can and do get winning results by using both styles. It is hard to argue with the record of some coaches who rely more on the coercive approach with their athletes and staff.

So, if we are arguing that the coercive approach is one you should avoid, how do some of the coaches who use this approach still manage to win? There are several possible explanations for their success. First, these coaches are usually very knowledgeable and competent in their sport. They know how to design great game plans that break down their opponents. Some people would argue that these coaches have been fortunate to coach very talented athletes who would probably succeed in almost any environment. Some would argue that fear is a powerful motivator—and it is. Athletes who play for coercive coaches will do almost anything to avoid being the brunt of their coach's tirades. Therefore, there is no denying that coercive coaches can get winning results from their athletes using this approach. However, as you will soon see, the overall benefits of going the credible coaching route infinitely outweigh coercive coaching.

"Pride is a better motivator than fear. I never wanted to teach through fear, punishment, or intimidation. Fear may work in the short term to get people to do something, but over the long run I believe personal pride is a much greater motivator. Remember, pride comes when you give respect."

John Wooden, Former UCLA Men's Basketball Coach

Questions for Reflection

- Do your athletes fear you or do they truly respect you?
- In what ways might you act like a coercive or credible coach?

Chapter Two Key Points

- The old command and control style of coaching is not the best way to motivate athletes.
- Credible coaching involves developing solid relationships with your athletes and motivating them through respect, encouragement, and trust.

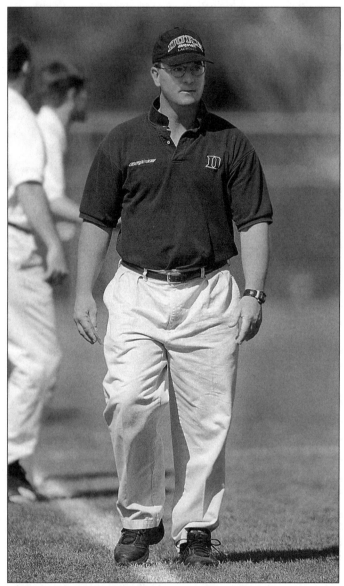

Mike Pressler, Head Men's Lacrosse Coach, Duke University

CHAPTER THREE

THE BENEFITS OF BECOMING A CREDIBLE COACH

"As your credibility as a leader rises, your followers will be more likely to respond in a positive manner to your actions."

Brian Billick, Baltimore Ravens

Nothing should be more sacred to you as a coach than your own credibility with your athletes. Whether you realize it or not, your credibility has an impact on every aspect of your program—that's why it is so important. Becoming a more credible coach is the key to unlocking and unleashing your team's potential. By improving your credibility with your athletes, you and your team will benefit in a multitude of ways, most notably the ones listed.

CREDIBLE COACHING IMPACTS AND IMPROVES. . .

Motivation and Commitment

Credible coaches create highly motivated and committed athletes. You have probably heard the phrase "I would run through a wall for coach." This saying epitomizes how strongly committed and compelled athletes can be when they are privileged to play for credible coaches. Athletes willingly work hard and go the extra mile for you when they believe that you have the ability to help them reach their goals. They also will give you their best effort on a regular basis when they see that you are committed to helping them be the best.

In contrast, coercive coaches create athletes who are at best compliant, but more often than not, resistant. Although compliant athletes might initially sound good because they will do what you tell them, it falls far short of the commitment that credible coaches inspire in their athletes. Compliant athletes will only do the the bare minimum to avoid the wrath of their coaches. Obviously compliance is not nearly enough to compete effectively. Today's highly competitive sporting world demands that people are fully committed to being the best. The only way you can truly tap into these levels of commitment from your people is by being a credible coach.

For example, a business study once estimated that 53% of lost productivity was due to poor leadership. Poor leadership leads to low morale, high absenteeism, poor quality work, apathetic attitudes, and a high turnover rate. In the sporting world, this translates to poor team chemistry, sloppy play, constant complaining, and athletes who are chronically late, miss practice, and look to transfer or quit.

Think of a past coercive coach, athletic director, or supervisor you had to endure. How did this person's ineffective leadership affect your motivation, commitment, and productivity? How did it affect your fellow teammates or coworkers? When there is poor leadership people look to survive, escape, or revolt. Those who seek to survive force themselves to do just enough to get by, but certainly not any extra. They show up physically but check out mentally. They go through the motions and show little passion or enthusiasm for their work. Their sport becomes a dreaded chore. They bide their time, hoping that things will somehow change, or a better opportunity will come along. Others look for opportunities to escape the situation. They either look to transfer or end up quitting altogether. Finally some people rebel against poor leadership. They criticize the leader and resist almost everything he is trying to accomplish. If things are really bad, sometimes people will even attempt to get their coaches replaced or fired. We all know of situations in which athletes have revolted and gone around their coaches in an effort to remove them. No matter how they respond, people who are subjected to coercive coaching have low motivation and little commitment. Ironically, sometimes they are actually more motivated to lose so that it reflects poorly on the coach. In a way, athletes who must endure coercive coaches consciously or unconsciously sabotage the team's success.

How much discretionary effort, commitment, loyalty, and respect are your athletes giving you right now? The vast majority of athletes will give you their best efforts provided you deserve it. Are you worthy of your athletes' best effort? You are worthy of it if they know they can trust you, which means you are credible.

Coachability

Did you know that your credibility and your athletes' coachability are interrelated? Think about it. If your athletes believe you are credible, they will intently listen to you and do what you say with enthusiasm. However, if they don't feel you are competent or have their best interest at heart, they will quickly tune you out.

Certainly there are some instances when the athlete's poor attitude is the major reason why he is uncoachable. You are going to have some bad apples every now and then. However, if you are credible the vast majority of the time your athletes will be coachable.

"Fail to honor people, they fail to honor you."

Lao-Tzu

Discipline

Here's a question for your to consider: What would your team do if for some reason you weren't able to tell them that you and your coaching staff could not make it to practice one day? How would your athletes react when they arrived at practice but you weren't there? Would they hang around for a while waiting to see if you were going to show and then go home? Would they organize themselves and begin practicing on their own as if you were actually there? Or would they race out of there as soon as you didn't show up on time and celebrate not having to practice? We know of a few coaches who, once a year or so, have intentionally arrived a few minutes late to practice just to see how their athletes would react. What would happen with your team?

Credible coaches are likely to find that their athletes would find a way to get in a quality workout regardless of whether or not their coach is present. Their athletes don't work out because they have to, but more so because they want to. Athletes of credible coaches clearly understand the importance of working hard to build their confidence and reach their goals.

Conversely, coercive coaches often have athletes who dread going to practice because it is not a fun experience for them. They often look to cut corners and will work hard only when the coach is watching. If a coercive coach did not show up for practice on time, the athletes would likely hang around for a while for fear that they would be severely punished if they left, but they probably would not begin practicing on their own. Instead they would likely celebrate not having to practice.

Credible coaches create athletes who are often self-disciplined. They are willing to work on their own and do not require constant supervision to ensure that they do their work. This is obviously a great benefit for coaches because of the limited time you can spend with each individual athlete. You can't monitor every weight work out, meal, or test.

Additionally, you can't always control the social decisions they make 24 hours a day. However, if they respect you, they will be much less likely to do anything to embarrass themselves or your program. Like children who respect their parents, your athletes will live up to the team's standards and follow the rules because they respect them and they don't want to disappoint you. In contrast, coercive coaches must maintain constant surveillance on their athletes in order to effectively control them.

Confidence

Because of their coaching style, credible coaches create athletes who play with confidence and trust their abilities. These athletes thrive in pressure situations because they know they are ready and that their coach believes in them. They trust their talents and play aggressively. We will discuss the numerous strategies credible coaches use to build their athletes' confidence in more detail in Chapter 8.

Recruiting

"I didn't want to go to a certain school because I found out that the athletes had no respect for the coach on my recruiting trip."

Division I soccer player

For those of you who recruit athletes, your credibility not only affects your current athletes but your prospective ones as well. As many coaches will attest, recruiting talented athletes is one of the biggest keys to success and the lifeblood of your program.

Recruiting is not an exact science. You can never tell what combination of factors athletes might use to decide where they will attend school. However, most recruits sign with the coach who they believe has the most credibility. They ask themselves, "Which coach will help me develop the most? Which coach has been honest with me? Which coach truly cares about me? Which coach believes in me and my potential? Which coach listens to me? Which coach do I trust? Which coach do I really want to play for?" Recruits often make their decisions based on the relationship with the coaches. Credible coaches have a certain charisma about them that attracts people to them.

Further, if you have built your credibility with your current athletes, they too will be a strong force in recruiting athletes to your team. In essence, they tell others what a great experience they have had and sell others on the program. In many instances, recruits commit to attend certain schools because the current athletes speak so highly of their coach. In other situations, the current athletes have flat out told recruits not to come to their school because they didn't want the recruits to be subjected to the coach's reign of terror.

Your Record

You can see that when you have athletes who are highly motivated, committed, coachable, disciplined, confident, and content, you will be much more likely to get them to perform to their potential. When your athletes give you their absolute best effort each time they perform, you are very likely to see more wins.

Your Satisfaction

The benefits of credible coaching do not just stop at wins. In addition to dramatically increasing your athletes' and team's chances of success, you will also receive a benefit that cannot be measured in your win/loss column, but is perhaps even more valuable. Credible coaching lets you enjoy coaching a great deal more. When you become a credible coach, you forge bonds with your athletes and connect with them as people. You build relationships that go beyond the mere teaching of sport skills to that of a mentor and guide who develops life skills. Your ability to have an impact on your athletes' lives for the long-term is quite possibly the most noble aspect of coaching. Most retired coaches don't miss the games; they miss the opportunity to develop strong and special relationships with people that coaching affords.

"I saw coaching as more of a mission. It provided me with an opportunity to make a difference in the lives of young people. This perspective gave coaching an added dimension of meaning and significance."

Tom Osborne, Former University of Nebraska Football Coach

"I suppose the obvious greatest satisfaction you receive is in winning the championship or winning the Super Bowl. But now, as I reflect, I cherish my relations with my players."

Bill Walsh, Former San Francisco 49ers Coach

"Basketball is just a game, but if I was doing my job as a coach that game of basketball would help our players by preparing them to do well in life, to reach their full potential as individuals. When they did that, I was very proud as a coach. That's more important to me than all the championships and titles and awards."

John Wooden, Former UCLA Men's Basketball Coach

Now that you know why your credibility is so important, let's examine how you can build it in the next chapter.

Questions for Reflection

- How would your athletes respond if you weren't able to make it to practice on time?
- How much effort, loyalty, and respect have you earned from your athletes?
- What do your athletes say about you and your program to prospective recruits?

Chapter Three Key Points

- Being a credible coach impacts your coaching in virtually every way.
- The more credible you are as a coach, the more motivated, committed, coachable, disciplined, and confident your athletes will be.
- Being a credible coach will not only dramatically increase your team's chances of being successful, it will also help you enjoy coaching more.

Mike Krzyzewski, Head Men's Basketball Coach, Duke University

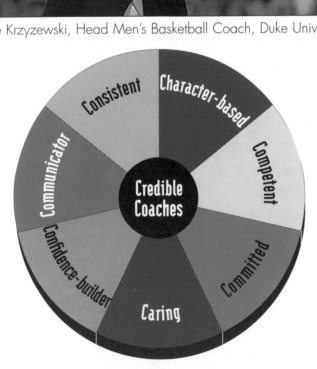

CHAPTER FOUR

THE SEVEN SECRETS OF SUCCESSFUL COACHES

How You Can Become A Credible Coach

"When one treats people with benevolence, justice, and righteousness, and reposes confidence in them, the army will be united in mind and all will be happy to serve their leaders."

Sun-Tzu, *The Art of War*

The Importance and Impact of Credible Mentors

In our Seven Secrets of Successful Coaches workshops and Championship Coaches' Academies, we often begin by asking coaches to reflect back on the people who they most respected during their lives and careers. We ask them, "Who are the credible coaches who have made a positive difference in your lives?"

It comes as no surprise that many of the people these coaches list were coaches they have played for or worked with during their careers. They might also be teachers, parents, brothers, sisters, friends, ministers, managers, and mentors of all kinds.

North Carolina men's basketball coach Roy Williams says, "I had three mentors in my life. My first mentor was my mother—she was my hero. She taught me to treat people the way you would like to be treated and to always do what is right. My second mentor was my high school coach Buddy Baldwin. Buddy was the first person to really give me confidence and he made me feel like I could be successful. More than anything, he gave me the idea of what confidence can do for somebody. In fact, because of his influence, he is the reason I decided to be a coach. And then there is Coach Smith. I think he's the best there has ever been on the court, but he is even better off the court. The players had such confidence and respect in how he was going to prepare them."

Indiana men's soccer coach Jerry Yeagley also believes his coaches were important in shaping his coaching philosophy. "My high school coach Barney Hoffman was sort of my early mentor. He was a little guy who was way ahead of his years in terms of the things he did with us and the experiences he gave us. And then when I was at West Chester, my coach, Mel Lauerback, was a very important mentor for me as well. Whereas Barney was more for the passion of the game and a real sensitive guy, Mel was a military guy who had every detail covered. He taught me an awful lot about administration and attention to detail and discipline. Those were the two most influential people in shaping my thoughts early on."

San Diego Chargers coach Marty Schottenheimer says, "Ed Hepe is the first guy who comes to mind as a mentor. He was my high school basketball coach in Pennsylvania. He created an environment of coaching and teaching that allowed every one of us to first and foremost feel good about ourselves and the contributions we were making to the team. The next guy was Joe Collier, the head coach at Buffalo. He was a great, great teacher and had an ability to communicate. He made me realize that preparation and planning lie at the foundation of any success you might have. Interestingly enough, the other person who had the greatest impact on my coaching philosophy was Bill Arnsbarger. Each of their personalities were very much the same. They were all soft spoken, never really lost control, never ranted or raved."

Tennessee women's basketball coach Pat Summitt still consults with her long time mentor Billie Moore. "She's the most professional person I have ever known. She taught me so much in terms of decision-making, what to look for in recruiting, and how to teach the game."

Credible Mentors Exercise

1. Take a moment and reflect on the people who you have admired and respected over the years. Who are the credible coaches and mentors in your life?

2. After you think about these people, go a step further to analyze what characteristics make them so respected and credible in your eyes. How did they communicate with you? How did they treat you? How did they handle various situations? What characteristics made them credible?

3. Note how you performed and felt when working with these coaches/leaders. What did you accomplish when working with these leaders and how did you feel about yourself under their guidance?

4. Now take a moment and think back to some coaches, bosses, managers, athletic directors, or other leaders who you did not trust or respect.

5. What were they like as leaders?

6. How did you feel and perform under their command?

You can often learn just as much from coercive coaches about what not to do as you can from credible coaches about what to do. For example, Arizona softball coach Mike Candrea learned some important lessons from one of his early coaching experiences. "I once worked with a coach who did not have very good people skills. He just didn't do a good job of stroking kids when they needed to be stroked. So I said to myself at the time that whenever I got my own program, I was going to be more positive-oriented. He taught me a lot more than he realizes." Many coaches who once experienced coercive coaches promised themselves that they would never treat their athletes the way their coaches had treated them.

The previous questions give you a chance to explore the role and impact that various leaders have had on your life. If you are like most coaches, these simple exercises gave you the opportunity to explore the qualities of credible and coercive coaches/leaders. Further, we are hopeful that reflecting on the credible leaders also touched an emotional chord within you. It is very likely that these people hold a very special place in your heart because they have made a profound impact not only on your coaching philosophy, but your life in general. Their credible leadership has formed the basis of who you are today as well as your ideal leadership style.

"I'm convinced that every successful coach has been profoundly influenced, for better or for worse, by every coach or teacher he (or she) has ever played for. The development of my own coaching style has been culled from the personalities and methodologies of numerous dedicated and talented men at various levels of the game."

Phil Jackson, Los Angeles Lakers

DISCOVERING THE SEVEN SECRETS OF SUCCESSFUL COACHES

We used many of the same questions you just answered when we asked coaches and athletes about what it takes to be a credible coach. Despite the fact that those we interviewed represented different sports, genders, and levels, the consistency of the people's responses cannot be denied. The same characteristics were repeated time and time again. We found that credible coaching can be organized into the following seven characteristics.

Credible coaches are...

1. Character-based

Credible coaches seek to do the right thing. They are honorable people with high ethical standards and great integrity. They tell the truth to their athletes and never manipulate or play mind games with them. They conduct themselves in a professional manner and take pride in representing their teams and athletes with class. Credible coaches look to surround themselves with people of solid character because they know that character is just as important as talent in the long run.

2. Competent

Credible coaches have a thorough understanding of the strategies and fundamentals of the game. They know how to make the appropriate adjustments and are seldom out-coached. Despite their solid understanding of the X's and O's, they are highly inquisitive people who continually look for innovative and improved ways of doing things. They are lifelong students of the game. Further, they understand that admitting their limitations and mistakes is actually a sign of strength, not weakness. While they are highly capable and often revered people, credible coaches also tend to remain humble and keep their success in perspective.

3. Committed

Credible coaches are highly committed people. They create successful visions for their teams and are more than willing to put in the time required to make them happen. They have a true passion for sport and coaching which fuels their intense drive and enthusiasm. They also have incredible reserves of energy and resiliency which enable them to weather the inevitable storms of adversity. Credible coaches are highly competitive people who really enjoy competing and winning at the highest levels.

4. Caring

Credible coaches care about their athletes as people. They sincerely want the best for their athletes in all aspects of their lives and are willing to help them in any way possible. Credible coaches invest the time to get to know each of their athletes on a personal level, showing an interest in their athletes' families, friends, faith, and future goals. Further, this caring does not end when a player's eligibility or career is over, but often extends throughout an athlete's lifetime.

5. Confidence-builders

Credible coaches continually build their athletes' confidence. They plant seeds of success in their athletes' minds and convince them that they can and will be successful. Credible coaches have a special knack for making people feel good about themselves and capable of achieving almost anything they set their minds to. They are demanding and set high standards yet are patient enough to help athletes develop and improve. When athletes fall short, as all of them eventually will, credible coaches use a good balance of being challenging and supportive to help people get back on track.

6. Communicators

Credible coaches are excellent communicators. They are open, honest, and direct when communicating with individuals and the team. They continually remind and refocus people on what they need to do to be successful. Credible coaches seek to involve their athletes as much as possible and value the input they receive from them. They have the remarkable ability to truly listen to their athletes. They take the time to understand where people are coming from and are able to make decisions accordingly. Because of their ability to listen, credible coaches often are aware of concerns and conflicts and proactively address these situations before they become major problems or distractions.

7. Consistent

Credible coaches develop a sound philosophy of coaching. This philosophy remains stable over time, but they are flexible enough to adapt to changing situations or times. Credible coaches bring a productive and consistent mood to practices and games, regardless of whether their team is winning or losing. They don't let the highs get too high or the lows get too low. Further, they maintain a consistent approach to the rules and standards of the team. They tend to have few rules, but are consistent in how they apply them whether a player is a starter or reserve. Finally, credible coaches tend to be highly organized people who take their practice and game preparation very seriously.

Credible Coaches are Complete Coaches

As the title of the book suggests, we have come to call these characteristics that credible coaches have in common the Seven Secrets of Successful Coaches. We chose the word "secrets" not because each of the characteristics is some kind of mystery. Rather, credible coaches possess the unique and elusive ability to live all of the characteristics at a consistently high level over time. Most coaches are proficient at some of the characteristics. For example they might have a good understanding of the game (competent) and are willing to work hard and put in the long hours (committed). But they might need some development in their listening skills (communicator) and their ability to be patient with athletes and help them feel good about themselves (confidence-builder).

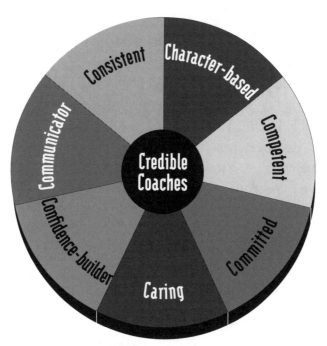

In contrast, the highly credible coaches we studied are able to blend all of the characteristics into a complete whole. It's not that credible coaches do only one thing right; they consistently do dozens of little things right on a daily basis. What we found is that credible coaches tend to be complete coaches. By this we mean that they are well-rounded people who have well-developed coaching philosophies. Credible coaches know who they are, what they want to accomplish, and what they stand for.

This is not to say that credible coaches are perfect people. They are the first ones to admit that they have shortcomings and areas which need improvement. Like every other coach, these coaches are human and do have flaws. They make mistakes, lose games, and some have even been fired at some time in their careers. However, while they know they are imperfect, they continually seek to be true to themselves and their athletes.

COACHING WITH YOUR HEAD AND HEART

In essence, what we have found is that credible coaches coach with both their heads and hearts. By combining these two important aspects, credible coaches become more complete, well-rounded, and effective coaches who are able to connect with their athletes.

Coaching With Your Head

Obviously, winning is important for both coaches and athletes. It comes as no surprise then that the credible coaches we studied had a strong desire to win and were extremely competitive people. These coaches had goals of winning conference and national championships and spent a great deal of time recruiting, practicing, and developing their teams so that they could perform at the highest level possible. In describing this aspect of coaching, we categorize coaches as being highly focused on their athletes' performance—in other words, they use their heads to create successful teams.

Coaching with Your Head Means:
- setting both long and short term goals.
- planning organized practices.
- training your athletes to execute the fundamentals of the game.
- scouting and analyzing future opponents.
- strategizing the X's and O's.
- making mechanical and tactical adjustments.
- analyzing videos of past performances.

Coaching with Your Heart

The characteristic that really set the credible coaches apart is their ability to coach with their hearts as well. Not only do they use their heads to focus the team on high level performance, they also spend a tremendous amount of time coaching with their hearts—building solid relationships and developing their athletes as people.

Coaching with Your Heart Means:
- developing quality relationships with your athletes.
- monitoring and improving your team's chemistry.
- building each individual athlete's confidence and self-esteem.
- being genuinely interested in your athletes' social, family, and personal lives.
- knowing how your athletes feel about their roles on the team.

- caring about their academic progress and goals outside of sport.
- being aware of and considering your athletes' emotions.

Credible coaches get to know their athletes as individuals. They regard their athletes as multi-faceted people with many goals, concerns, fears, and frustrations outside of their athletic role. By investing the time to show your athletes that you care about them as people, they will feel that you are looking out for their best interests and, in turn, they will be more willing to extend their loyalty back to you.

Overcoming the "Tyranny of the Or"

Unfortunately, there are some people who believe that a coach must choose between coaching with his head or heart. They mistakenly believe that if you focus on the head aspects that you cannot achieve the heart aspects, and vice versa. For example, a sports writer once wrote an article about a coach insinuating that the coach could not consistently win because he cared too much about his team. The headline of the article actually read "Here is the Choice: A Winning Coach or A Caring Coach." This sports writer could not have been more off base. To suggest that a coach must make a choice between winning or caring about his athletes is absolutely crazy. It is this very belief that keeps so many coaches and athletes from achieving their potential. This belief is also an insult to the many coaches featured in this book and around the world who win because they care about their athletes.

This limited "either/or" thinking falls in line with what business authors James Collins and Jerry Porras of *Built to Last* call the "tyranny of the or." Basically this means that people mentally limit themselves by falsely believing that they can have only one choice but not both. The authors studied high level businesses and found that the best businesses were able to care about their people and achieve high profits. This head and heart approach to business is a big reason why companies like Southwest Airlines, Ben and Jerry's Ice Cream, Federal Express, and Starbucks are *Fortune* 500 companies as well as being consistently listed as the *Fortune* Top 100 companies to work for.

"FedEx, from its inception, has put its people first both because it is right to do so and because it is good business sense as well."

FedEx Manager's Training Guide

"We created an environment where we pay attention to them, their personal lives as well as their business lives. We wanted to show them that we don't just regard them as work automatons. We wanted to create an environment where people can really enjoy what they are doing. People know whether you are treating them this way for some kind of purely economic reason or whether you're doing it because you like people and value them."

Herb Kelleher, CEO of Southwest Airlines

Leading with Your Heart

It seems that the majority of coaches focus much of their time on coaching with their heads. They get consumed with the X's and O's and mechanics of the sport. They watch countless hours of film, fine tune mechanics, and get bogged down by paperwork. Because of this they often neglect the heart aspects. However the heart factor is the edge. Coaching with your heart is so critical that Duke men's basketball coach Mike Krzyzewski titled his book *Leading with the Heart.* Coach Krzyzewski says, "It's important for a leader to focus on the technical aspects of his industry or business. But it's vital to focus on details related specifically to people in the organization." In other words, the head aspects are important for leaders, but the heart aspects are critical. Credible coaches recognize the importance of both and are able to strike an appropriate balance between the two. When you coach with both your head and your heart, you develop athletes who play with their heads and hearts.

"To measure a leader, put the tape around his heart, not his head."

John Maxwell, Author of *Developing the Leader Within You*

"A lot of coaching is people skills. You must build a relationship with your players. Not for only three or four years, but a lifetime relationship."

Mike Candrea, University of Arizona Softball

Questions for Reflection

- What have you learned about leadership from the credible coaches you played for or worked with?
- What have you learned about leadership from the coercive coaches you played for or worked with?
- How do you rate on each of the seven secrets of successful coaches?
- How much do you coach with your head and how much do you coach with your heart?

Chapter Four Key Points

- Learn lessons from both the credible and coercive coaches you played for or worked with.
- Credible coaches share seven characteristics. They are character-based, competent, committed, caring, confidence-builders, communicators, and consistent.
- Credible coaches are complete coaches because they coach with both their heads and their hearts.

MIKE KRZYZEWSKI

Head Men's Basketball Coach
Duke University

Three-time National Champions
Three-time National Coach of the Year
Naismith Basketball Hall of Fame

On Character

The most fundamental thing about being a good leader is the ability to communicate in a trustworthy manner. If you do that on a consistent basis, the element of trust is developed, which is the cornerstone on which every coach-athlete relationship should be built.

Coaching is about relationships. It goes way beyond X's and O's. You have to create an environment of trust among your staff and athletes. Without trust, you have nothing. If you do have trust, you will be able to accomplish great things.

On Commitment

A leader can't ask anything of those he or she is leading that he or she is not willing to do as well. As a leader you have to do it really well—at a much higher level than anyone else.

On Caring

I think you show someone you care about them by being willing to listen to them. There is no better way to show you care than to give them time. Certainly if you develop programs that will help them academically, you talk to them about their personal lives, you handle their training properly, you handle their nutrition properly, you remember their birthdays, you know their parent's names, you know their girlfriend's name, you will show that you care.

The key word for all of this is empathy, not sympathy. On a day-to-day basis we all have pressures we have to deal with. You have to try to understand their world. Basically having empathy shows that you care.

On Confidence Building

If an athlete knows you believe in him or her, then when that kid goes through dark moments, he or she will know they are not alone. We all have those moments and it is important to know that others are with you. Our guys know that they are never alone because we develop relationships and let them know we believe in them.

Do you get on them for mistakes of omission or commission? We get on guys for mistakes of omission. I will really get on people who don't concentrate or those people who don't play hard. You have to create an environment where people can make mistakes without worrying about it so much. If they are concentrating and playing hard and make a mistake that is different than if their heads are in the clouds.

What do you do after you get on an athlete? That is important. If I have really gotten on someone, then I am going to have an assistant grab that kid after practice and show him what he did on tape and explain to him why I did what I did. It isn't a singular event. You have to follow up with the explanation.

On Communication

A good leader listens—and more so than that, gives time to listen. The bigger the leader, the busier the leader, the harder it is to take the time to listen. You have to get it in your mind that you have to listen-that there couldn't be any time better spent than listening.

On Consistency

I have found that the more precise I am in setting rules, the more you become a slave to the rules and not really doing things that are pertinent to the individual or team you are working with. You become an administrator of rules rather than a leader. So the first thing is to not have too many rules.

Mike Candrea, Head Softball Coach, University of Arizona

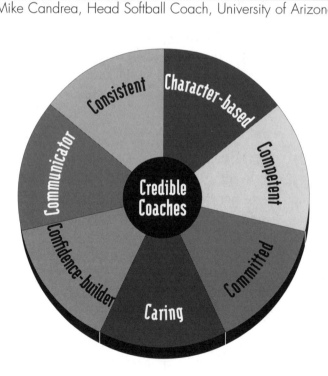

CHAPTER FIVE

HOW YOUR CREDIBILITY EVOLVES AND DEVELOPS

"I think through the years my philosophy has changed. I was very result-oriented early on in my career and after I won that first championship, I think I became a better coach because I became more well-rounded. I see a lot of coaches who are so obsessed with winning that first one that they tend to lose track of the big picture."

Mike Candrea, University of Arizona Softball

COACHES DEVELOPMENTAL STAGES: THE TYPICAL EVOLUTION OF CREDIBILITY

You might have noticed that the majority of the coaches we featured in this book are in their mid 40's to mid 60's. Many of them certainly began their coaching careers with some of the characteristics of credible coaches, however, their evolution into a more complete and credible coach took time, a lot of soul searching, and experience.

Looking back over his coaching career, former Nebraska volleyball coach Terry Pettit can trace the evolution of his coaching philosophy. "I coached for 23 years and I think the first eight years I was definitely a developing coach; the second eight years I was a pretty good coach; and my last eight years there is no question I was a much better coach in all facets than I was before."

Like many things in life, a coach's philosophy evolves over time. Many coaches admit it takes a good 10 years of evolution before they arrive at a coaching philosophy that is comfortable for them. Ask most coaches and they will tell you that they approach things differently after years of experience than they did their first season, and rightly so. Through trial and error, learning from mentors, reading books, attending clinics, and talking with fellow coaches, a coach's philosophy and style develops over time.

New York Yankees manager Joe Torre is a great example of a coach whose philosophy evolved after several years of coaching. After getting fired three times in previous jobs, he credits attending a personal development seminar as the catalyst to changing his approach to become a more credible coach.

As a result of observing and talking with coaches for several years now, we have identified typical developmental stages that coaches experience during their careers.

1. Survival Stage

As the name suggests, a coach's primary focus in this initial stage is simply to survive and eventually advance. Typically these are assistant coaches at the middle school, high school, and college levels and the parents or teachers at the youth levels who are relatively new to coaching. While occasionally these coaches may think they know all there is to know, they have much to learn not only about the game itself but also all the other responsibilities which go along with coaching.

The two major mistakes we see in this stage center on friendship and power. On the friend side, some coaches in the survival stage are concerned that they must be liked by every player at all times. In an effort to be liked, they often avoid challenging athletes enough and let them get away with things they shouldn't. As North Carolina women's soccer coach Anson Dorrance says, "I think one of the great mistakes that all the young coaches make as they are entering the profession is the feeling they have to be liked. And what ends up happening is they end up trying to win a popularity contest, and they end up sacrificing the respect of the team."

On the other hand, some new coaches feel that the only way they can get respect is by forcing it upon the athletes. These power hungry, insecure coaches try to impose their methods on athletes with the thought that toughness equals control. However, as we have said, respect must be earned from your athletes, not forced upon them.

"The whole learning process of 27 years was really a trial from the beginning. I had never conducted a practice when I got the job. I was 22 years old and in a panic. I remember watching the first game and I was clueless about what the other team was doing because I could only see us. I just had a very narrow focus and I think it was a 'my way or the highway' mentality."

Pat Summitt, University of Tennessee Women's Basketball

"You know I thought I had all the answers when I first started coaching and now after thirty years I realize I didn't know much at all."

Jerry Yeagley, Indiana University Men's Soccer

2. Striving for Success Stage

In the second stage, coaches focus on building a winner and making a name for themselves. Coaches in this stage spend long hours developing their programs so that some day they can compete with the elite teams for championships.

In this stage, many coaches look to take traditionally poor or mediocre teams and build them into contenders in a relatively short period of time. If they can do this, the reward is often a more prestigious and higher paying job at another program. In essence, coaches look to find athletes and build programs that will help them climb the career ladder.

These coaches are often very driven to prove that they are good coaches, not only to their colleagues but also to themselves. The potential problem with this striving for success stage is that sometimes coaches are primarily concerned with their own personal success and not always the welfare of their athletes. Be careful not to use your athletes as the rungs on your ladder to success. Athletes can tell whether you are in coaching for the right reasons or in it for yourself.

"As a young coach I was more interested in personal accomplishments. I think this is normal. You are just starting out in your chosen career and you're trying to prove yourself. You tend to see the world in terms of 'I.' Your focus tends to be on your goals, your own ambitions, your own successes, your own world."

Rick Pitino, University of Louisville Men's Basketball

3. Significance Stage

Coaches in the significance stage not only seek success for their programs, but equally as important, they seek to have a significant impact on the personal lives of their athletes. These coaches play to win but they also have the perspective to understand that the most important game their athletes will ever play is the game of life.

For example, Duke men's basketball coach Mike Krzyzewski emphasizes education so much to his players that he will not hang a championship banner until the seniors in the program graduate. Despite winning championships, Coach "K" does not feel his job is finished until his players achieve success both on and off the court. Coach Krzyzewski says, "If the only reason I coached was to win college basketball games, my life would be pretty shallow. I coach not only because I love it, but because I have the chance to teach and interact with young people."

Credible coaches are significant because they value their athletes as people. In doing so, they build strong bonds with athletes that last beyond a person's playing career. Their athletes seek their counsel not only to become better athletes but also better people.

"Once you get a little older, and you start to attain a certain measure of individual success, you start to realize that the only true success is group success; that true greatness is the ability to make those around you better. This usually doesn't come in some great epiphany, one magic moment of sheer insight when you realize the error of your ways. Instead, it's usually a gradual process, evolving over time, until one day it is in front of you as clear as day."

Rick Pitino, University of Louisville Men's Basketball

"At first it was very important to win and I felt I needed to do whatever it takes to win. Now I am still as competitive as ever and I want to win as much as ever, but now the more important rewards for me are the relationships."

Jerry Yeagley, Indiana University Men's Soccer

"Try not to become a success, but rather try to become a person of value."

Albert Einstein

4. Satisfied Stage

A fourth stage that we have seen some coaches enter is what we called satisfied. This stage tends to happen after coaches have reached their goal of winning a championship. Or it also can happen when a coach finally gives up the goal of winning a championship after several years and becomes content being a little above .500. In this stage, coaches tend to lose their intense drive, passion, and competitiveness. They don't work quite as hard as they used to and display less enthusiasm for the job. It's almost as if they go through the motions and put in the time necessary, but fail to be totally committed.

Although this stage might be comfortable for the coach, ultimately it is doing the athletes a disservice because they are being led by someone who is settling for mediocrity. We all know of coaches who are in the satisfied stage. They have hung on after winning a championship and aren't willing to put in the continued work and dedication to stay there. Or they have abandoned their chase for the top and have settled for being in the middle of the pack. Either way, it is human nature to eventually become satisfied and content.

5. Spent Stage

The spent stage is when a coach is burned out. Unfortunately this stage is not that uncommon and has hit such notable coaches as Dick Vermeil and Dick Bennett. Because coaching is such an intense and demanding profession, coaches are very susceptible to burn out. With challenging and selfish athletes, cut-throat recruiting, impatient administrators, fickle fans, biased parents, budget constraints, and meddling media, it's no wonder that coaches get frustrated and fed up with coaching.

Coaches who find themselves in this stage need to do some serious soul searching. Hopefully after reading through this book and talking with some colleagues, you will find a way to rekindle your passion for coaching as well as effective ways to minimize the stresses and demands. Or you might find that it is time to get out of coaching and put your energy into a new direction that is more fun and fulfilling for you.

How Average and Credible Coaches Evolve

Based on these stages, we have seen that average coaches and credible coaches differ in their development. Average coaches tend to experience all of the stages for varying amounts of time whereas credible coaches spend a great deal of time in the significance stage and many times can avoid both the satisfied and spent stages.

Average Coach

Survival (1-3 years), Striving for Success (3-20 + years), Satisfied (2-10 years), Spent (1-5 years)

Average coaches start out spending one to three years in the survival stage. Once they get a feel for what they need to do, average coaches then spend a great deal of time in the striving for success stage chasing championships. It is during this time that the outcome of winning a championship often clouds their perspective. They become so obsessed with winning that it is easy to act more like a coercive coach than a credible one.

If these coaches achieve the championship they so desperately desire, they often move into the satisfied stage because they feel they have done what they needed to do to prove themselves. After a while of being satisfied, they get burned out on coaching and eventually retire or leave the profession.

Credible Coach

Survival (1-3 years), Striving for Success (2-5 + years), Significant (10-25 + years)

Credible coaches usually begin their careers much like average coaches, but follow a much different path. Most credible coaches do start in the survival stage as they figure out what coaching is really all about. Then, because they are young, they too tend to get transfixed by winning and making a name for themselves. However, as they formulate their coaching philosophy they come to understand that winning is not everything nor the only thing. After a few years of blindly pursing championships, most credible coaches also come to realize the importance of developing positive relationships with their athletes. It is this people first approach, or coaching with your heart as we called it earlier, that eventually helps coaches have a much better chance of winning the championships they so desperately desire in the success stage. It is this same credible coaching approach that allows coaches to enjoy coaching much longer and helps them avoid feeling satisfied or spent.

Shortening Your Learning Curve

The important lesson in examining these stages is to determine where you are now in comparison to where you would like to be. One of our primary reasons for writing this book was to both speed and shorten your evolutionary process as a coach. Instead of waiting until you are 10, 15, or even 20 years into your coaching career before you realize that credible coaching is the best way to go for your professional and personal success and satisfaction, we want coaches to gain these important insights at a much earlier point in their careers.

Thus, if you are a beginner coach in the survival stage, keep in mind that there is a lot to learn. If you are in the striving for success stage, realize that coaching with your heart will dramatically increase your chances for success. Plus it will give you and your athletes a chance to enjoy your sport even more. In doing so, you will enhance your chances of success by becoming a coach whom athletes respect, not just in sport but throughout the rest of their lives. For those of you in the significance stage, continue developing winners in sport and the game of life. If you are in the satisfied stage, we challenge you to either renew your commitment to excellence or consider whether it is time to hang up your whistle and give someone else with more passion a chance to lead. Finally, if you find yourself in the spent stage, do some serious soul searching to see if you might be able to rekindle your love for coaching. If not, find something else you would rather be doing and go for it—life's too short to be miserable.

Questions for Reflection

- What was your philosophy when you first started coaching?
- Which developmental stage would you say you are in now?
- In which developmental stage would you like to be?

Chapter Five Key Points

- Your coaching philosophy will develop and evolve over time.
- Credible coaches focus on making a significant impact on their athletes.
- If you can focus on being a coach of significance, you can often avoid becoming complacent or burned out.

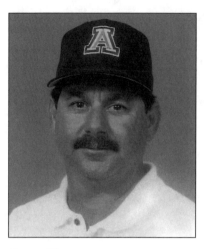

MIKE CANDREA

Head Softball Coach
University of Arizona

Six-time National Champions
Three-time National Coach of the Year
NFCA Hall of Fame

On Character

I think kids are going to reflect the head coach. If you look at successful programs you are going to probably find more head coaches who are more well-rounded.

As I've matured a bit and gotten older, I evaluate the season on a lot more things than just winning or losing. I think that has been a big change in my career. When I was young that was it—we either did or we didn't. Now you sit back and evaluate and say, "I think this team gave me everything they had."

On Competence

The minute you quit trying to become the very best teacher of the game is the day you should quit. You should know your game backwards and forwards.

On Commitment

Coaching takes a passion. I think once that passion starts leaving you I think most people know that it's time to get out of it.

On Caring

I think a lot of coaching is the relationship you build with the kid. If you build an open relationship where kids are more apt to talk you can learn a lot. One thing I have realized is that you can't change a personality so you have to understand it and be able to adapt to it. Or try to get that person to work with you and not against you. And I think the more you do that, the better the relationship becomes.

I work very hard at getting to know my players well enough that if something is bothering them, that is the most important thing for me at that moment. Because if I don't deal with that, practice and the game and everything else is irrelevant.

I always try to talk to every kid at least once every day about something other than softball. I think that's what helps build trust and the kind of relationship that it takes to get kids to that next level.

On Consistency

As a young coach, one of the biggest mistakes I made was after a game where we would get beat. I would air it out, sometimes to the point that I couldn't even remember what I said, but I felt better. Then, afterwards, I would regret what I said because I didn't really have time to think about it. Now, if I don't have anything positive to say, I wait 24 hours.

Pat Summitt, Head Women's Basketball Coach, University of Tennessee

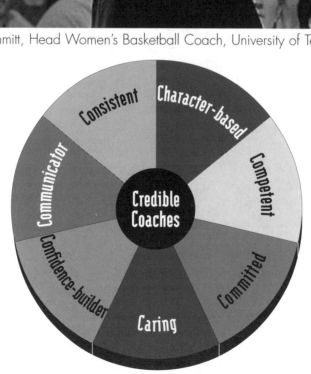

CHAPTER SIX

COULD YOU PLAY FOR YOURSELF?

Five Steps to Becoming a Credible Coach

"Leaders need introspection. Knowing yourself—your strengths, your weaknesses, and your values—is essential."

Rick Pitino, University of Louisville Men's Basketball Coach

Are you the coach you would like to be? Although you are probably proud of many aspects of your coaching, virtually every coach has areas in which he or she would like to improve. This chapter along with the rest of the book provides you with an opportunity to reflect on, assess, and strengthen your coaching skills and philosophy. In doing so, you will maximize your potential as well as the potential of the athletes you coach.

Regardless of what sport, level, or gender you coach; whether you are a head or assistant coach; whether you are a beginning or veteran coach; what your past record might be; or what your present coaching philosophy might be, we hope that these beginning chapters have made you think about your approach to coaching and sold you on the overall value of becoming a more credible coach. Fortunately, you can choose to be a more credible leader. In the words of former Green Bay Packers coach Vince Lombardi, "Contrary to the opinion of many people, leaders are not born. Leaders are made, and they are made by effort and hard work."

Despite the overwhelming benefits, along with Coach Lombardi we must advise you that becoming a more credible coach is anything but an easy task. It requires a great deal of effort and awareness, as well an open mind. As we have already mentioned, rarely is it something that can be done overnight. Rather it is an ongoing process which evolves over time. Just like an athlete who is trying to improve her sport skills, you will have many breakthroughs as well as occasional setbacks. Therefore you should be patient with yourself as you work through the process.

Keep in mind that the toughest rule with credibility is that it takes time to build but can be destroyed almost instantaneously. Building solid relationships with each of your athletes requires time and effort. It can take weeks and months to earn your athletes' trust and respect. However, one damaging lie, cutting criticism, act of unfair favoritism, or indiscretion can destroy your credibility immediately and sometimes irreparably. Therefore you must treat your credibility as if it were a sacred, delicate, and priceless treasure—because it is just that.

Inside-Out Approach

If you truly want to be more of a credible coach, you must make it an inside-out approach. What this means is that you can't become a credible coach just by superficially learning a set of techniques or strategies. Instead, you must align your core coaching philosophy to be that of a credible coach. You can't just act like a credible coach—you must be one. Credible coaching must form the foundation of your coaching philosophy so that it emanates from the inside out to your attitudes and actions. Credible coaching is who you are, not something you do.

Credible coaching really begins by being able to understand and lead yourself first. You must understand your motives, strengths, and shortcomings before you can try to influence and change others. We will provide you with a variety of strategies to better understand yourself as a leader in the upcoming assessment section.

Be Yourself (Unless You're a Jerk)

In a similar quest, author Debra Benton has spent much of her career studying the best CEOs of major American companies. One of her best pieces of advice in her book *How to Act Like a CEO* is to "Be yourself, unless you are a jerk." This humorous yet truthful statement definitely applies to becoming a more credible coach.

We ultimately want you to be yourself. While it is likely that you may make some adjustments to the way you approach your coaching as you read this book, we strongly encourage you to be yourself. We do not recommend that you become an exact replica of Gail Goestenkors, Mike Candrea, Mary Wise, or Marty Schottenheimer. This would be both impossible and fraudulent. We merely hold up these successful coaches as exemplary and familiar models to guide your journey to becoming a more credible coach. To successfully reach this goal, you must be yourself and work from your strengths while minimizing your weaknesses. You have to figure out who you are and see how you might be able to adapt the leadership principles we advocate into your personality and coaching style. Remember, we want you to be the best coach you can possibly be—not a clone of someone else.

Florida volleyball coach Mary Wise says that when she first began coaching at the the age of 22 she tried to be like her college coach Carol Dewey. "Early on I was just trying to be like Carol Dewey who I had played for at Purdue. Slowly I realized that I had to be me. I couldn't try to be somebody else. I think as young coaches we do that. You try to be who you mentored after. And yet I think the most successful coaches are those whose personalities fit their system."

Duke women's basketball coach Gail Goestenkors admits that she too started off emulating what had been done at Purdue when she was an assistant. "When I first came here (Duke), I ran all the offenses and defenses we ran at Purdue because that is what I was comfortable teaching. It wasn't the best thing for us to do because we only had eight players. But that's what I was comfortable with and I wanted to be in a comfortable place so that I looked like I knew what I was doing. And, in retrospect, we should not have been doing some of those things."

Fortunately, the seven secrets of successful coaches can accommodate a variety of coaching styles. Although the coaches we feature have similar philosophies and principles, their styles are very different. Nebraska softball coach Rhonda Revelle, who has spent time with and observed three of the credible coaches mentioned in the book, puts it this way, "Mike Candrea's personality is very different from Terry Pettit, which is very different from Tom Osborne. Yet they have found a way to be the best in their sport." Thus, you still can maintain your style and personality as you adapt the principles to your philosophy.

"To be an effective leader, we must work within our own personalities. There are many coaching styles and techniques that are successful. But we become confident and successful when we take information from others and make it work within our style. We need to put our own signature on it."

Rhonda Revelle, University of Nebraska Softball

A FIVE STEP APPROACH TO IMPROVING YOUR CREDIBILITY

We want to provide you with a step-by step process that will help you assess, improve, and strengthen your credibility. This process will give you the opportunity to gauge your present credibility in a variety of ways. Next it will help you pinpoint your current strengths as well as your areas for improvement. Then you will have an opportunity to build on your strengths and target some of your areas for development. Finally, you will be presented with a wealth of practical ideas to help you enhance your credibility with your athletes.

1. Assess Your Credibility
2. Recognize Strengths and Target Areas to Improve
3. Gain New Skills, Strategies, and Insights
4. Practice and Use Them
5. Get More Feedback

1. Assess Your Credibility

You can assess your credibility in a variety of ways. We encourage you to first rate your own credibility. Then strongly consider having your athletes rate your credibility as well for a more complete and accurate measure.

Assessing Your Credibility on Your Own

- "Would You Play For Yourself?" Reflection
- Rate Yourself on the Seven Secrets of Successful Coaches

"Would You Play for Yourself?" Reflection

One of the more powerful ways to assess your own credibility is to reflect on and honestly answer the following question: "Would you play for yourself?" Imagine being an athlete who plays on your team. Would you be motivated to give your best? Would you respect and trust you? Where would your confidence be if you were your own coach? Would you develop to your full potential if you were coaching yourself?

Taking the time to reflect on the hypothetical question of "Would you play for yourself?" is a very powerful exercise. If the question causes you some uneasiness, embarrassment, or regret, now is the perfect time to become a more credible coach. If you would have a hard time playing for yourself then it stands to reason that your athletes may feel the same way.

"I don't know if I could have played for myself early on."

Pat Summitt, University of Tennessee Women's Basketball

"As a manager you must ask yourself, 'Am I someone who I would want to work for?'"

Bill Logue, Senior Vice President, FedEx Corporation

Credible Coaching Self Assessment

A second way to evaluate your own credibility is to rate yourself on the Seven Secrets of Successful Coaches using a one to ten scale. This short self test will help you analyze your strengths as a coach as well as your areas for improvement. Be sure to be completely honest with yourself.

Credibility Self-Assessment

Using a scale from one to ten,
rate yourself on the following characteristics:

Strongly Disagree	Disagree	Agree	Strongly Agree
1 2 3	4 5	6 7	8 9 10

☐ 1. **Character-based**—I act in an ethical, honest, and trustworthy manner.

☐ 2. **Competent**—I have a solid understanding of the rules, mechanics, and strategies of my sport.

☐ 3. **Committed**—I work hard and am committed to building a successful program.

☐ 4. **Caring**—I genuinely care about my athletes and their overall success.

☐ 5. **Confidence-builder**—I am effective at building and maintaining my athletes' confidence.

☐ 6. **Communicator**—I am an effective communicator and listener.

☐ 7. **Consistent**—I am consistent in terms of my mood and my approach to team discipline.

Rarely has any coach given him or herself a perfect score on all of the characteristics. You will find that you have some strengths as well as areas to improve. Reflecting on and rating your credibility provides you with a good starting point.

Have Your Athletes Assess Your Credibility

"Coach really does care what we have to say. I will tell you that several of my friends play on teams where their coach would never ask their athletes for feedback about how the coaches were doing or how the program was being run. I respect coach a lot for allowing us to do that."

NCAA Division I Women's Basketball Player

Keep in mind that your credibility is ultimately evaluated by your athletes. They are the true judges of your effectiveness. You might be able to trick yourself into thinking that your athletes respect you, but as the saying goes, you can't kid a kid. Because your athletes are the ultimate evaluators of your credibility, they are the best people to help you assess where you stand.

Having your athletes give you honest feedback on your effectiveness might sound like a scary and vulnerable proposition to some coaches. But you will obtain no better or accurate appraisal of your credibility than by directly asking your athletes.

Think of it this way. How much feedback do you give your athletes regarding their performances over a typical season? If you're like most coaches, you are continually providing them with suggestions, corrections, and compliments. The vast quantity and quality of the feedback you give them is designed to help them improve their performances. Imagine if you never provided your athletes with any feedback whatsoever, either positive or negative. How well would they develop and improve? Obviously they would not improve near as much without your feedback. Thus if feedback is so important for your athletes, it is equally important for you.

Asking for Feedback is Like Visiting the Dentist

Receiving feedback from others regarding your effectiveness or the effectiveness of your program can be a difficult exercise to conduct. Credible coaches are willing to receive feedback because they are comfortable enough with themselves to allow others to evaluate them. It takes a certain amount of confidence to put yourself "out there" for others to evaluate.

Asking your athletes for feedback on your coaching has been compared to visiting the dentist. Most people are apprehensive about going because they are unsure about what the dentist might find. Even though they might be given a clean bill of dental health, they fear the potential pain and expense they might have to face. Some people are so scared that they procrastinate making appointments or worse yet never go. While they might be able to put off the possibility of experiencing some minor pain in the short term, if they avoid the dentist for too long, they will be very likely to make the situation worse and eventually experience severe pain and possible tooth decay and loss in the long run. However, those who get regular checkups and cleanings are able to maintain great dental health and keep their smile for many years.

Like visiting the dentist, when you ask your athletes to assess your credibility, you risk discovering that they think you are a credible coach and are doing a fantastic job or that you may need some minor or major work on your coaching. If you continually put off asking for their feedback, you assume an even greater risk that could eventually cause your team to decay, or worse yet, lose them altogether, both figuratively and literally. Thus, taking the preventative approach by getting occasional credibility checkups will keep both you and your athletes smiling in the long run.

There are several ways you can obtain feedback. To get informal feedback you might meet with your captains on a regular basis. You might have a team council made up of at least one representative from each class that you meet with regularly. Or, you might have a time at the end of one practice each week where you meet with the entire team to get feedback about how practices and other aspects of the program are going. To get more formal feedback, you might allow your athletes to evaluate you and the program anonymously.

For example, most major businesses are now having employees rate the effectiveness of their managers and supervisors. The process is often called

360 Degree Feedback because supervisors receive feedback on their leadership skills from everyone around them—employees, peers, and supervisors. The feedback they receive is primarily used to help them become more effective leaders. On some occasions, the feedback is even used to determine promotions and raises.

In addition to your athletes, consider asking your assistant coaches, athletic director, and any support staff you might have (managers, trainers, academic advisors, peak performance consultants, strength coaches) to rate you as well. Their insights will provide you with an even better measure.

Protect Your Athletes' Anonymity and Confidentiality

If you decide to ask your athletes to rate your credibility, the process must be anonymous and confidential. Your athletes will not be completely truthful with you if they think their identity or comments might be revealed in any way. Therefore it is best to have an objective and trusted person, other than yourself, handout, collect, and tally your athletes' responses.

In addition to your athletes trusting there will not be negative consequences for their honesty, they must feel that you will sincerely consider their feedback and make changes when appropriate. This is not to say that you must change everything they suggest. But, we are suggesting that you at least consider their feedback and be willing to modify certain aspects of your coaching style or the way the program is run if your athletes indicate it will help them perform better. You will be amazed at the respect you will earn if you are willing to listen to their feedback, honestly evaluate it, and make positive changes based on that feedback.

Like you did with yourself, you can simply ask your athletes to rate you on a one through ten scale on each of the seven characteristics. Be sure you have evaluated yourself before you have your athletes evaluate you.

Credibility Athlete Assessment

Using a scale from one to ten,
rate your coach on the following characteristics:

Strongly Disagree			Disagree			Agree			Strongly Agree		
1	2	3		4	5		6	7		8	9	10

☐ 1. **Character-based**—My coach acts in an ethical, honest, and trustworthy manner.

☐ 2. **Competent**—My coach has a solid understanding of the rules, mechanics, and strategies of my sport.

☐ 3. **Committed**—My coach works hard and is committed to building a successful program.

☐ 4. **Caring**—My coach genuinely cares about me and my overall success.

☐ 5. **Confidence-builder**—My coach is effective at building and maintaining my confidence.

☐ 6. **Communicator**—My coach is an effective communicator and listener.

☐ 7. **Consistent**—My coach is consistent in terms of his/her mood and approach to team discipline.

Authors' Note: We have developed a more detailed 360 Degree Feedback survey called the Credible Coaching Questionnaire.™ The 28 item questionnaire provides you with a thorough and specific assessment of your credibility. If you would like more information on using this comprehensive questionnaire, please contact us.

Interpreting Your Athletes' Feedback

When you receive the composite information, it is important that you look at it as a way to improve yourself. Your first tendency is to look at the lower scores and either try to rationalize them, deny them, or figure out who gave you the lower scores and plot your revenge against them. This is certainly not what we recommend. Instead, compare the ratings you gave yourself on each of the seven secrets with those of your athletes. You will likely find similarities as well as differences. Remember that the ratings your athletes have given you are based on their perceptions of you. You may not agree with some of them, however it's your athletes' perceptions of you which determine how they respond to you. Thus, whether or not you agree with them is beside the point—their perceptions become your reality.

Note any areas where you athletes gave you higher ratings. These are areas that your athletes see as strengths. Take a moment to reflect on why your athletes might see these areas as strengths for you. What is it that you are doing to make them strengths? Then note any areas where your athletes gave you lower ratings. These are your areas to improve. Again take a moment to reflect on why your athletes might view these as areas of improvement for you. What are you doing now that makes them an area of concern for your athletes?

If you are willing, we suggest you consider sharing your results with someone you trust and who has your best interest at heart. This could be another coach, peak performance consultant, a friend, or your spouse. This person can help you make sense of the ratings if you are uncertain about any of them as well as serve as a sounding board to help you process the information. (We will talk more about the importance of developing a Peer Resource Team in the next chapter on Character.)

Be sure to thank your athletes for providing you with their honest feedback. You don't need to tell them much more than that unless you want to. By opening yourself up to their feedback, you have already made a huge first step in showing them that you value their input.

2. Target Areas to Improve

Once you have gone over your athletes' feedback, you next need to target some areas you would like to improve. While we encourage you to read the entire book from start to finish, you can go directly to the specific chapters which highlight the areas you would like to improve.

3. Gain New Ideas and Insights

Each chapter will provide you with a wealth of proven strategies to become a more credible coach. As you read each chapter, see what ideas and insights you might be able to incorporate into your coaching strategy.

4. Practice and Implement Them

Try your new coaching strategies with your athletes. Perhaps you will begin having regular meetings with your athletes to find out how they are doing. Or you might work on paraphrasing what your athletes say before giving your response. Whatever the case, the credible coaching strategies you are using should have at least a subtle if not significant impact on your athletes.

5. Get More Feedback

After two to three months of using your new strategies, have your athletes rate you again to see if there is any kind of change in how your coaching is perceived. Ideally you will see improvement in the areas you have targeted.

Going back to our dentist analogy, we suggest that coaches get credibility checkups roughly twice a year. Schedule a checkup about one third to one half of the way into your season and the other soon after your season is finished. These periodic checkups will help you effectively monitor your credibility and help you address potential problems before they have more serious, long-term consequences.

Questions for Reflection

- Are you the coach you would like to be?
- Do you truly understand why you coach?
- Are you being yourself or are you trying to be like someone else?
- Could you play for yourself?
- How do you rate on each of the Seven Secrets of Successful Coaches?
- Are you willing to have your athletes assess your credibility? If not, what is holding you back?
- If you receive any less than favorable feedback from your athletes, can you focus on the lessons rather than dwelling on it or getting discouraged by it?
- Are you as committed to improving and developing yourself as a coach to the same level that you ask your athletes to improve and develop themselves?

Chapter Six Key Points

- Becoming a more credible coach is a challenging task but one that is well worth the effort.
- Becoming a credible coach is an inside-out approach. You must understand and work within your own style and personality. Above all, you must be yourself.
- Becoming a more credible coach begins by having you assess your strengths and areas for improvement.
- The most accurate way to assess your credibility is to ask your athletes for their feedback.
- Once you assess your current credibility, acknowledge your strengths, target your weaknesses, develop a plan to gain and practice your new skills, and then reevaluate.

PAT SUMMITT

Head Women's Basketball Coach
University of Tennessee

Six-time National Champions
Seven-time National Coach of the Year
Naismith Basketball Hall of Fame
Women's Basketball Hall of Fame

On Character

The players need you to be real. And I am very real. I always tell them that winning doesn't give you the right to think that you're better than someone else and losing doesn't make you a bad person. You have to keep life in perspective and it's never as bad as it seems, nor is it as good as it seems.

I think you have to establish your philosophy. I don't think you can try and be four different coaches. You have to arrive at what's really important to you.

I think as a coach it's vital that you lead by example. I'm a teacher and if I want them to understand our philosophy then it's up to me. If I want them to be on time, I'm on time. If I want them to have good communication skills, I have to have good communication skills.

You have to surround yourself with good people and people who are on the same page as you. They're not going to undermine you; they're going to be incredibly loyal to you and committed no matter what your philosophy might be. You have to have that loyalty and support.

On Commitment

I expect our teams to work just like I do. They know I'm here early and I stay late. I watch film with them. Whatever it takes. If they want to shoot extra, I'm here.

On Caring

I really think first and foremost you generally have to care about the people you work with. I don't think you can fake that. I think it's got to be real and the reason I love so much what I do is that I get the opportunity to work with people. You develop those relationships and if I didn't care then I wouldn't be doing this. I could work in a factory and look at a machine all day, instead of looking in the eyes of the 17, 18, or 19 year-olds and trying to get them to be better than they are at that time or better than they really believed they could be.

On Communication

Kids today want to know 'why are we doing this coach?' And that's okay. In my first five years they were afraid to ask.

When I was a young coach, I would just react instantly to a situation. I used to not be able to leave a locker room without getting upset after saying exactly what was on my mind. Now I can go and say "Good win," even if I wasn't pleased and let them enjoy the win. And then the next day at practice I'll say, "Ladies let me tell you exactly how I feel about the way you played yesterday."

I don't want to know everything. I tell our kids, "I don't want to know everything." If they can handle it then I tell them to handle it. You come to me when you really think I need to step in. You need people who you can trust.

On Consistency

Our philosophy is to be firm, be fair, but be consistent. Players really watch for coaches who favor their best players. I've never really had a problem with that. I like people. I'm not about titles; whereas a lot of people are about titles. I'm friends with the custodian and the president of the university. It's just people and there's a right way and a wrong way to treat people and that's true with discipline.

Marty Schottenheimer, Head Football Coach, San Diego Chargers

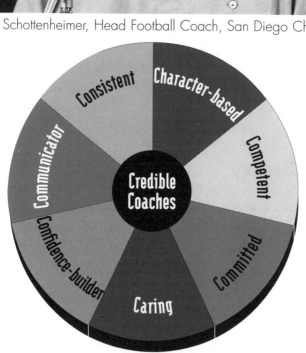

CHAPTER SEVEN

Credible Coaches Are
CHARACTER-BASED

How To Build A Sense of Trust With Your Athletes

"Leadership is a potent combination of strategy and character. But if you must be without one, be without strategy."

General H. Norman Schwarzkopf

Imagine yourself in the following scenario. You and your team have made it through the regional playoffs and have earned the right to play for the national championship. It's 6:30 a.m. and you and your players are at the airport for an early morning flight to the site of the championships. As your players are checking their bags, you discover that one of your All-American players violated a major team rule the night before. What do you do?

Do you let it go this time because, after all, she is one of your best players and you are playing for the national championship? Or do you enforce the team rules that were established at the beginning of the year and suspend her for the rest of the playoffs? You realize that suspending her now would really hurt your team's chances of winning the championship. However if you don't suspend her you might lose the respect of your team. To further complicate the matter, the local media is also at the airport to get your last comments before you board the plane. If you suspend her now, the media could turn this into a very embarrassing situation. What would you do?

Arizona softball coach Mike Candrea once found himself in this exact situation. With his team's chances of winning a national championship on the line and the media looking on, Coach Candrea said the following, "Take her bags off of the plane. She's staying home. We are going without her."

Coach Candrea stuck to his principles and his word when he made the decision to leave his star player at home. He did this because he would rather risk losing a championship than risk losing self-respect and the respect of his team. Despite not having one of their best players, the team pulled together and actually won the championship. To this day, Coach Candrea believes that sticking to his principles has been a big key to his program's success, both short and long term.

Character is the Foundation of Credible Coaching

In our work with athletes, we have found that the overwhelming majority of them want a coach with character and integrity. They want someone whom they can be proud of, respect, and trust. They say things like: "We want a coach we can respect, one that will do things with honor and integrity," "We want a coach who is going to do the right thing," "We want a coach who will be honest with us and tell us the truth," and "We want a coach who doesn't manipulate us or play mind games with us."

We have chosen to focus on the concept of character first because we are convinced that it is the foundation for all of the other characteristics you need to be a successful coach. While all of the characteristics are certainly important, a lack of character can be the most disastrous for you and your athletes. As we begin this discussion, we would like for you to consider the following questions. Is it really important for a coach to have character to be successful? What does it mean when athletes say they want a coach who has character and integrity? What comes to your mind when you think about being a coach of character? These are just a few of the questions we hope to help you answer as we discuss the concept of character.

The Difference Between Your Reputation and Your Character

If asked, you would most likely say that you would like for people to consider you a person of integrity and character. Most of us would say the same thing. But, sometimes there is a difference between how people perceive us and our true character. In our society and particularly in the coaching ranks, reputation is very important. Administrators, fellow coaches, athletes and others involved in your sport rely heavily on your reputation to judge whether or not you are worthy of holding a certain coaching position. How closely aligned are your reputation and your real self? Are you the same when no one is watching you? How about when you know you will not get caught? John Wooden sheds some light on the difference between reputation and true character.

"Character is who you really are; reputation is what you are perceived to be."
John Wooden, Former UCLA Men's Basketball Coach

As you read this chapter on character, we hope you will take a close look at yourself and honestly evaluate whether or not the important people in your coaching life (e.g., athletes, colleagues, administrators) know the real you.

What it Means to Have Character

In our interviews with credible coaches, we have found that they demonstrate their character in three primary ways. First, they understand their principles and are not willing to sacrifice them for wins. They put their convictions over what is convenient. Secondly, credible coaches are extremely honest people. They refuse to lie to or manipulate people. Third, because they understand that a person's character is so important, credible coaches use it as a key factor when recruiting and selecting athletes and staff.

"A lot of our success in Duke basketball has to do with character. And at the heart of character is honesty and integrity."
Mike Krzyzewski, Duke University Men's Basketball

Seek To Do the Right Thing

"I want a coach who won't do anything to get us in trouble. Our coach now is very good about that. So we don't have to worry about it with him."

High School Football Player

"I didn't want to go there because they have a bad reputation for cheating. The athletes who go there are seen as thugs."

College Basketball Player

It is safe to say that the majority of us want to do the right thing in most situations. However, we don't always do the right thing. Character means that you not only know what is right in a particular situation, you are also willing to do what is right no matter the consequences. In other words, you don't worry about how much you might personally gain or lose as a result of a particular decision. There is no doubt that doing the right thing is worth it. The trouble is that most coaches know the right thing to do. The difficult part for them is doing it because of the pressures to win.

Take a few minutes to read the following scenarios and determine what you think is the appropriate action to take for each. As you consider your response, think about what you would do, not what you think other people would want you to do.

1. As a head coach, one of your assistants tells you that two of your "star" athletes are allowing someone else to write their papers and do their assignments for them. You investigate and learn that it is true. What do you do? Do you take immediate action to stop this infraction and discipline the athletes? Do you ignore the situation and hope that no one finds out about it. Or, do you rationalize that you need these players to win and it really isn't hurting anyone?

2. As a college coach, you have a scholarship athlete who is in his/her third season of eligibility. This athlete came in with a very good recruiting class and works hard in practice. However, the athlete has seen very little playing time. In your mind the athlete has not contributed very much to your program. You feel you need to have

a successful season in the upcoming year to maintain your job security. While you are interested in recruiting several athletes who play other positions, you do not have any scholarships available. Do you let this athlete keep the scholarship and finish out his/her eligibility? Or, do you find ways to take the scholarship and give it to someone else you feel might help you win more?

3. As a college coach, your team is competing at another school. One of your top players has a final exam scheduled during the time the team is supposed to be away from campus. The professor in the class has agreed to allow you to administer the exam once you arrive at the hotel. The exam is placed in an envelope and you put it in your brief case. Once at the hotel, you tell the athlete to stay in the room and you are going to make sure the other athletes are beginning their workouts. You leave the room and come back a few minutes later. You notice that your briefcase has been opened and the envelope containing the exam is open as well. You confront the athlete and he says he just "glanced" at the test. If you turn the athlete into university authorities, there is a good chance he will be dismissed from school. Do you tell him he was wrong, keep him from competing and report him to school authorities? Do you tell him he was wrong, let him take the exam and punish him by making him run extra in practice when you get back on campus? Or, do you tell him he was wrong for looking at the test, but do nothing else about the situation?

What would you honestly do in these three situations? Most of us know the right thing to do in all three situations. The problem arises when it comes to doing the right thing. And when the "rubber hits the road," we have to have the character to do the right thing. Because coaches are faced with situations like these on a regular basis in sport, it is important to have a philosophy of coaching that addresses your convictions and provides you with some guidance when you are faced with potential ethical decisions.

"If you don't have principles and standards as a coach it's too easy to sell your soul to the devil."

Fred Harvey, Head Track Coach, University of Arizona

"You must know your philosophy and convictions as a coach because you will be tested."

Joe Gibbs, Washington Redskins

Have you taken the time in recent months to reflect on your philosophy of coaching? How long has it been since you asked yourself questions regarding the principles you feel are important for you to follow as a coach? Do you have a written philosophy that guides your decisions on a daily basis? Have you thought about the legacy that you want to leave regarding your character and integrity when you are finished coaching?

"The legacy I want to leave is doing things the right way, doing things ethically, doing things morally, and being competitive and fiery, yet classy. Would I love to win a national championship? Absolutely! And is it something I dream about? Absolutely! But I won't do it at all costs. I won't sell my soul for a national championship."

Rhonda Revelle, University of Nebraska Softball

"The bottom line is that if you've been able to clearly identify with your values as a coach, with what is important to you, and you've demonstrated that from day one, it seems that those are the teams that are playing late into the season."

Tom Renney, Director of Player Personnel, New York Rangers

"It's not hard to make decisions when you know what your values are."

Roy Disney

In working with highly credible coaches, we have found that they have a philosophy of coaching and use it as guide for the decisions they make. Credible coaches know what they stand for and try to live their philosophy on a daily basis. They place principles over winning at all costs. They are unwilling to sell out long-term success, satisfaction, or principles for short-term gains. Credible coaches are aware that victories can be very hollow if they are at the expense of bending rules, at the expense of using athletes or being less than honest with them. If you have not done so, we encourage you to take some time to write down your philosophy of coaching. Or if you have a written philosophy, make a commitment to revisit that philosophy and determine if you are living by the principles you have written.

While going through this process, ask yourself some of the following questions:

- Is winning at all costs the way I want to operate? Or at what cost do I want to win?
- What kind of influence do I want to have on the athletes I coach?
- How do I want my athletes to remember me in terms of my character?

Once you have addressed these questions, take some time to plan a course of action that will encourage you to live your philosophy on a regular basis. In other words, what are you going to do today to make sure your legacy as a coach of character is being realized? Keep your philosophy statement in a place where you can review it often.

An Ethics Checklist

In addition to your philosophy statement, you might consider the following questions offered by Russell Gough in his book *Character is Everything: Promoting Ethical Excellence in Sport.* Use these questions as a guide when you are faced with a difficult situation and you are not sure of the choice you should make.

1. Is it against the rules?

-Of the game, my conference, or the law?

2. Is it fair to everyone involved?

-To my opponents, team, game officials, school, or myself?

3. Would my ethical role models do it?

-Who are my ethical role models? Do I have the courage to do what they would do?

As Gough encourages, you should probably ask yourself these questions in order, especially if you are dealing with a concrete rule. Do you really need to go any further down the list if it is against the rules? Also consider that if you say "no" to any one of these questions, you probably have the answer you need.

4. How will I and those I care about feel about this decision?

A fourth area to consider as part of your ethics checklist is "How will I and those I care about feel about this decision?" Here are a few more ideas to help you determine what is the right thing to do.

The Newspaper Headline Test

Another simple way of determining what is right and wrong we call the Newspaper Headline Test. Simply, if what you plan to do was a headline in the USA Today newspaper the next morning, would you be proud of it? If the answer is yes, then it is probably something you should do. If the answer is no, then it is likely you should not do it.

The Family Test

Similarly, the Family Test really hits home for a lot of coaches. Imagine having to explain the decision you made to your son, daughter, spouse, mom, or dad. Ask yourself, "Would I be proud to tell my family about how I handled the situation?"

The Mirror Test

Finally, the Mirror Test is another easy one to use. Basically, stand in front of a mirror. As you look yourself in the eyes ask yourself, "Can I really feel good about the decision I am about to make?" Again, the answer to this question will point you in the right direction.

"There is no pillow as soft as a clear conscience."

John Wooden, Former UCLA Men's Basketball Coach

Develop Your Own Peer Resource Team

Because there are so many gray areas in sport and coaching, former Nebraska volleyball coach Terry Pettit strongly encourages coaches of all levels to develop their own Peer Resource Team. A Peer Resource Team is a small group of people who are genuinely interested in you and can serve as trusted advisors when you need to make difficult decisions. They can be a sounding board for your ideas. They can help you sort out your conflicting thoughts. They can allow you to vent your frustrations. And they can give you support and keep you sane during times of stress. A Peer Resource Team is a specialized collection of people you can count on to help you survive and thrive in the up and down world of coaching.

Coach Pettit says, "I think that a Peer Resource Team is particularly important when a coach is in crisis and there may not seem to be any clear decisions—so there aren't any best decisions. It is a matter of trying to find a better decision and you have that sounding board that probably can keep you from making a bad decision."

Take a moment to assess who your Peer Resource Team might be—your spouse, assistants, former coach, friends, peak performance consultant, clergy? Coach Pettit suggests developing a well-rounded group of three or four people. He suggests that one person be someone who knows the technicalities and demands of your sport. This could be another coach in a different conference or level of play. Another person should have some background in psychology and/or human performance. Obviously this could be a peak performance consultant, counselor, or social worker. Finally, another member of your Peer Resource Team could be a spouse or very close friend.

If you don't already have your own formal or informal Peer Resource Team, invest some time in developing one for yourself. It will go a long way in helping you handle the hassles and headaches of coaching as well as help you become a more respected and credible coach.

Seeking to always do the right thing is the ideal you should strive to achieve. But you should also realize that all coaches fall short and rationalize some decisions. This doesn't mean that you don't have credibility. It just means you are human. As long as you are working towards being a coach of character, you will have more credibility with your athletes.

Tell the Truth: Honesty is the Best Policy

"A coach has to be honest with his or her athletes. I have had several coaches in my career who have lied to me for various reasons. You talk about losing credibility, those coaches lost my respect right away when they lied."

College Football Player

A second aspect of character that athletes want from their coach is to tell them the truth. They want a coach who will be honest with them and follow through on what is said. They don't want empty promises. They would rather you not say anything if there is a chance you cannot follow through on your promise. Athletes might not always like what you have to say, but they will certainly respect you more in the long run if you are open and honest with them. When it comes to the importance of coaches telling the truth, the two areas that athletes mention the most are recruiting and the roles they play on your team.

Honesty in Recruiting

For those coaches involved in the recruiting process, it is important to be honest with prospective athletes and avoid making empty promises. One of the fastest ways to lose credibility with your athletes is to make a promise while recruiting and then not deliver on that promise. A promise that is often made to athletes is that they will start right away if they come to a particular school. Sometimes, this promise can be fulfilled. But if there is a chance you might not be able to follow through, don't say it.

One athlete told us his personal experience with a coach who made empty promises during the recruiting process. This particular athlete arrived at school his freshman year and was rooming with one of his teammates who happened to play the same position. One day their discussion revolved around how they decided on this particular school. It turned out that both athletes were promised they would be the starter at the same position. The coach in this situation clearly made promises he could not possibly deliver. That coach lost credibility with those two athletes before the season ever began. It was difficult for either one of them to believe their coach from that time forward.

Tom Osborne, the former football coach at the University of Nebraska, says that you have to be honest with kids in the recruiting process. They have to know they can trust you and that your word means something. Sometimes, telling the truth will cause you to lose a prospect that can really help your team win immediately. Dean Smith, the former men's basketball coach at the University of North Carolina lost highly rated point guard Kenny Anderson to Georgia Tech because he would not promise him a starting position his freshman year. Coach Smith was not going to promise something he didn't know if he could deliver.

If you recruit prospective athletes, make sure you are "up front" with them from the very beginning. When you recruit you are essentially "selling" the benefits of your school. And, the pressure to bring in great recruits is something that all coaches live with every day. But, at what price do you try to get kids to commit to your school? Turn the tables for a second and think about when you go shopping for something that is really important to you. What happens when you are sold a product and the salesperson makes promises about the particular product that aren't true? How much will you trust that person in the future? Will you go back to him or her for future purchases? Will you doubt that person's integrity? Athletes ask themselves similar questions about the coaches who recruit them.

"I want our team to know that when I tell them something, it's the truth. They have to know that my word is good. I don't know if there is a bigger issue for me. In the long run, I believe most people will respect and appreciate someone who's honest with them."

Mike Krzyzewski, Duke University Men's Basketball

Honesty When Determining Team Roles

It is also imperative that you are honest with athletes when defining their roles on your team. Some coaches don't take the time to define athlete roles on a team. However, the importance of this will be addressed further in Chapter 9 on Communication. But assuming you do communicate with athletes about their roles, they deserve to be told the truth. Many times the athlete's view of what his or her role on the team should be is going to be different from the way you view it. And, sometimes it is very difficult for certain athletes to accept a role that is not what they expect. The key is for you to be able to get all of your athletes to "buy into" their roles and reach their potential within those roles. To begin this process, you must be honest with them. Even though some of your athletes will not like what you have to say, they will respect you more in the long run if you level with them.

Gail Goestenkors, the women's basketball coach at Duke University, says it's very important for her to be brutally honest with her players about the roles they have on her team. She has an individual meeting with each player early in the season and lets the athletes know which "piece of the puzzle" the player represents in the success of the team. In addition to telling each athlete where she fits into the scheme of the team, Gail provides her with feedback on ways to change that role if she is not happy with it. This is a key aspect of this process because she gives the athlete concrete aspects of her game to work on to improve her role if she isn't happy with it.

"The single most important obligation you have to your athletes is to be honest with them. They aren't always going to agree with your decision or think it is fair, but it is your obligation to be honest with them."

Marty Schottenheimer, San Diego Chargers

Most coaches don't intentionally misrepresent themselves, the team or an athlete's situation. However, it is important to remember that athletes don't forget. A well-respected college coach told us of a situation when he promised a kid he would get to play in an upcoming game because he had been practicing really well leading up to the game. The game began and this kid believed he was going to play because of his coach's promise. As it turns out, the game did not go as planned and the coach didn't feel like he could play him. Nothing was ever said about the situation until the athlete was ready to graduate. In his final meeting with this senior, the coach asked him if there were any suggestions he had that would make him a better coach. The athlete replied that he didn't appreciate what happened to him that day as he felt like the coach lied to him. He never forgot that situation and the coach lost some credibility with him on that day. The coach learned a valuable lesson from that situation and works very hard to always follow through on what he says or explain why he wasn't able to follow through.

Emphasize Character With Your Athletes

For those coaches who have the opportunity to recruit or select their athletes it is important to look for athletes who demonstrate qualities of character. Michael Josephson, founder of the Josephson Institute of Ethics and the program Character Counts, says that we should care about the character of the people with whom we choose to associate. He says that if we know their character, we can better predict how they will respond to adversity, temptation, and success.

Many coaches overlook an athlete's character in the selection process, especially when they are in the success stage we mentioned before. Because they want to win, some coaches knowingly recruit talented athletes with questionable character. Even though they don't completely trust the athlete and realize that he or she is likely to be disruptive to the team's chemistry, too many coaches gamble on questionable athletes solely because of their talent. While they might be successful in the short term, unfortunately in many cases these choices come back to haunt them and the team.

"When I drafted on talent, looking the other way regarding character, I have been burned almost every time."

Don Nelson, Dallas Mavericks

"If you don't have good people first and foremost in your dressing room, it will be a long season."

Tom Renney, Director of Player Personnel, New York Rangers

"Although I realize that I'm not going to win in the NFL without some extraordinarily skilled players, character has always been just as important to me—and in some cases, more important.

Don Shula, Former Miami Dolphins Coach

Many successful coaches say that an effective way to assess an athlete's character is to watch how she treats her parents. Arizona softball coach Mike Candrea says, "When recruiting players, I always look to see how they treat their parents. It's a great way to tell a lot about their character." If an athlete treats her parents with disrespect, it is very likely that she will eventually do the same to you. However, if she treats her parents with respect, she is probably a person of solid character.

Tennessee women's basketball coach Pat Summitt also uses an athlete's transcript to gauge her character. In addition to a player's grades, Coach Summitt looks at how many days a player may have missed school. She says she actually stopped recruiting a player because the athlete had missed 15 days of school in one year without a major illness. She knew that this player's lack of discipline would not be a good fit for her program.

"I work incredibly hard to recruit talented people with character. Not just great moves, but great character. Not just great shooting, but a great person. And you have to be selective because when you start out sometimes I think you might want to bend a little bit and take a chance. And I don't ever want to lower my standards because of someone's great talent."

Pat Summitt, University of Tennessee Women's Basketball

Developing Your Athletes' Character

For those of you who do not have the option of selecting the players on your team, it is important to help develop character in the athletes you are given. Rick McGuire, a sport psychologist and Head Track and Field Coach at the University of Missouri, emphasizes this in his workshops with youth and high school coaches. During his workshops he asks coaches to think about the lessons or skills they hope their athletes will develop or enhance as a result of being a part of their program. This is a great question and we often ask the same question of coaches who attend our coaching workshops. When asked, coaches will say they want their athletes to learn things like teamwork, self-discipline, responsibility, and a good work ethic. One characteristic that inevitably comes up is character. Coaches say they want their athletes to learn the importance of character and integrity. Our next question to the coaches is, "What are you doing on a daily basis to ensure your athletes are learning these important life skills?" We try to emphasize that athletes will not develop these skills just because they are playing a sport. For example, there are many instances (like cheating or displaying bad sportsmanship) where athletes have the opportunity to display poor character in sport. As the coach, you have to make it a point to emphasize the importance of character and provide opportunities for them to develop this important trait.

The following poem titled "The Guy in the Glass" provides a nice summary of the importance of being a coach who is character-based.

THE GUY IN THE GLASS

When you get what you want in your struggle for self,
And the world makes you King for a day,
Then go to the mirror and look at yourself,
And see what that guy has to say.

For it isn't your father, or mother, or wife,
Whose judgment upon you must pass.
The fellow whose verdict counts most in your life
Is the one staring back from the glass.

He's the fellow to please, never mind all the rest,
For he's with you clear up to the end,
And you've passed your most dangerous, difficult test
If the man in the glass is your friend.

You may be like Jack Horner and "chisel" a plum,
And think you are a wonderful guy,
But the man in the glass says you're only a bum
If you can't look him straight in the eye.

You can fool the whole world down the pathway of years,
And get pats on the back as you pass,
But your final reward will be heartaches and tears
If you cheated the man in the glass.

Dale Wimbrow

Questions for Reflection

- Are you honest with your athletes?
- Do you follow through on what you say?
- Do you emphasize the character of an athlete as much as talent?
- What are you doing on a daily basis to ensure your athletes are developing strong character?

Chapter Seven Key Points

- Always be open, honest, and direct when communicating with your athletes. Remember, they won't always agree with your decision, but they deserve to be told the truth.
- Develop an Ethics Checklist and a Peer Resource Team that will help you make tough decisions.
- Conduct yourself in a professional manner and take pride in representing your team.
- Surround yourself with people of solid character.

MARTY SCHOTTENHEIMER

**Head Football Coach
San Diego Chargers**

On Character

Let me tell you this. The single obligation, not responsibility because there are lots of responsibilities that you have as a coach, is honesty. You have an obligation to be honest and beyond that you have no obligation. It is not a responsibility. It is an obligation.

When things are going well, you can win with anyone. When things aren't going well, the only way you can win is with people who have character. When all of the negative things begin to occur because you are struggling, the guy with character will be able to withstand that far better than the individual that doesn't have character. A classic illustration for me was in KC, my final year there I made choices regarding people that were wrong. I abandoned some of the basic principles I had always believed in and exercised. I know why I did it. It was from the frustration and the inability to get to the championship. I had done everything else. The other part of it that relates to what I was talking about before regarding character, is that as coaches we all feel like we can manage people. The good ones probably can, but there is a limit to the number that you can manage. And what happened in KC is that we ended up with too many of those cases. I became a maintenance guy rather than a football coach. I wasn't a leader, I was a manager of all of these problems. No one else created these problems but me. That frustration and realization of the situation was a major reason for my decision to retire. I had compromised some things that I had always believed in. I learned from that and it will never happen again.

On Caring

The relationships that are developed are the most important part of this whole thing. Some people are so immersed in the business that they lose a sense of the personal. But you know something, ultimately the satisfaction you get from the personal side far exceeds anything else. I use this illustration. The number of games I have won, I don't keep track of. I could get a record book and look it up. But, that is what record books are for. But let me tell you something, you don't have to go into the record book to see the satisfaction of achievement on a young man's face after you have been working long and hard with him. You don't have to have a record book to determine whether you are a success. If you help a kid be able to be confident in himself and accomplish some things, that is what is all about.

On Confidence Building

I don't know what you gain from ranting and raving at players. They don't want to hear me ranting and raving. My job is to teach them in that moment and they aren't going to hear me if I am ranting and raving. I can get angry from time and time and vent. But that doesn't really help us win. I think for young coaches the best thing you can do is first find out if the young man knew what happened. Because he may not know what happened. That would be the best advice I could give. Go out and find out what the player's thoughts are on the situation before you go ranting and raving at him. If you include them in the solution, it really helps you.

On Consistency

There is one coach in the NFL who says, "The better the player, the better I treat him." I couldn't do that. I don't think that is the best way to handle things. I have always said that it is everybody or nobody. My point is that everyone should be given the same opportunity to feel they are important.

The cornerstone of any relationship is trust. You can apply that to any relationship you have. You have to trust that you are after the same things. What honesty and consistency do is develop a level of trust. If you can develop that level of trust, then you can endure the tougher times easier and increase your chances of being successful.

Mary Wise, Head Volleyball Coach, University of Florida

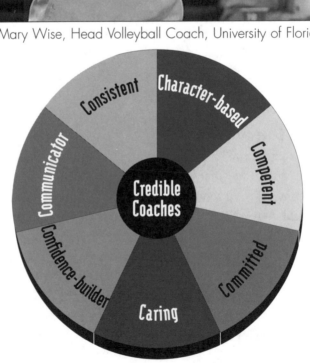

CHAPTER EIGHT

Credible Coaches Are COMPETENT
You've Gotta Know Your Stuff

"He who knows, yet thinks that he does not know, has great wisdom. He who does not know and thinks he knows is diseased."

Lao-Tzu

While your character is at the core of being a credible coach, few athletes will follow you if they don't believe you are competent. You must have a solid understanding of the skills and strategies of the sport. Your athletes must feel that you know what you are talking about when you coach them, determine the lineup, implement game plans, and make adjustments. If your athletes do not feel like you know what you are doing, they will be highly unlikely to truly listen to you let alone follow your advice. Therefore, your competence as a coach is another critical component of your credibility.

What are the most important factors that athletes use to judge your competence? Do your athletes believe you are competent? If not, how can you build your competence? In our discussions about competence with athletes and coaches, we discovered that there are three primary areas that contribute to competence. The first is your overall knowledge and understanding of the game. The second is your ability to keep up to date with the latest innovations of your sport as you seek to stay on the cutting edge. And the third, ironically, depends on your ability to willingly admit your faults and fallibility. Let's take a look at each of these areas in more depth.

Credible Coaches Know the Game

"He really knows his stuff. I have had several coaches since him, but none know the game like he does. The great thing about him is that he not only knows it, he can teach it."

College Football Player speaking of his Middle School Coach

Competence obviously implies knowledge. As a coach, you must have a solid understanding of your sport in three primary areas—the rules, mechanics, and strategies. Knowing the rules is an obvious must. Nothing destroys your credibility more with athletes, officials, opposing coaches, and fans than not knowing the basic rules of the game. Of course, there will be times in your career when a bizarre situation will occur and you might not know all the technicalities of the rulebook. Your players will forgive you in these situations because odds are none of them knew the rule either. However, if you do not understand the basic rules of the game, we strongly suggest you put down this book for now and turn your attention to a rulebook.

Competence also means that you can teach your athletes the correct mechanics for the game. In most sports, there are a variety of physical skills to be learned and mastered, many according to the positions people play. Therefore, credible coaches often need to be adept at teaching a variety of sport skills. Not only must you be able to teach the basic and advanced mechanics, but you must also have a keen eye to spot mechanical flaws and make the proper adjustments. Competent coaches have a thorough understanding of the physical skills necessary to perform as well as an arsenal of drills and methods to teach and refine these skills.

In addition to knowing the sport skills, you must also have a complete understanding of the strategies and tactics of your sport to be deemed competent. You need to able to devise a comprehensive and well thought out game plan to defeat your opponents offensively and defensively. This requires the ability to analyze the strengths and weaknesses of your team and implement strategies and plays appropriate for your personnel. You'll notice that while successful teams tend to have basic offensive and defensive philosophies that are consistent from year to year, they will also make some adjustments to maximize their strengths and minimize their weaknesses.

Not only do you need to find a system that works for your team, you also must analyze and devise ways to disrupt your opponents. Competent coaches intensively scout their opponents and create intelligent game plans that take them out of their game. Credible coaches are excellent at spotting an opponent's Achilles Heel and designing a winning game plan to exploit it.

While competent coaches must do a lot of work in preparing their athletes to execute a game plan ahead of time, the truly successful coaches are also able to make smart and quick strategy adjustments within competition itself. Duke men's basketball coach Mike Krzyzewski estimates that a coach's ability to make the proper adjustments within the game itself probably makes a significant difference in about 20% of games each year. While this number might not seem like a lot at first, imagine giving yourself 20% more wins each year or, worse yet, 20% more losses. This is often the difference between being a conference champion, making the playoffs, or winning a championship.

Knowing is Not Enough

Not only do you need to know a lot about your sport to be considered competent, but more importantly, you also must be able to successfully deliver your knowledge in practical ways that can be easily understood and applied by your athletes. Like some college professors who are geniuses in their subjects but put their classes to sleep when they lecture, there are some absolutely brilliant coaches in terms of the X's and O's who can't effectively relate what they know to their athletes. Great coaches are great teachers. A telltale sign of great coaching is that their athletes show noticeable improvement from the beginning of the season to the end of the season, and certainly throughout their careers. Great coaches infuse their knowledge into their players so that the knowledge eventually becomes part of the athlete.

"No coach ever won a game by what he knows, it's what his players have learned."

Amos Alonzo Stagg, Former University of Chicago Football Coach

Competence Outside the Game Itself

Additionally, in today's world, coaches are increasingly asked to assume a variety of duties to maintain a successful program. These areas of competence often go beyond the game itself and include such areas as fund raising, public relations, public speaking, budgeting, athletic training, and strength training. While you might not consider these areas as critical to your success, these related competencies are receiving increased attention by athletic directors and administrators when hiring and retaining coaches. Thus, coaches are expected to be competent in areas outside of just traditional coaching as well.

Assessing Your Competence Exercise

Take a moment to assess your competence in the following areas related to coaching. Mark the areas where you feel you are sufficiently competent with a "C." Use an "I" to signify areas that you would like to improve. Use a "D" for areas that you can delegate to an assistant or support staff member, and an "NA" for any areas which may not apply to your situation.

_____ Offensive strategy	_____ Managing conflict
_____ Defensive strategy	_____ Equipment
_____ Technique/mechanics	_____ Organizing/Scheduling
_____ Strength training	_____ Recruiting
_____ Conditioning	_____ Promotion
_____ Nutrition	_____ Fund-raising
_____ Motivation	_____ Injury care/Rehab
_____ Team Building	_____ Facilities maintenance
_____ Stretching	_____ Statistics
_____ Others_____	

Upon finishing the exercise, if you have discovered any important areas where your competence is lacking or you don't have someone who you could successfully delegate it to, we encourage you to invest the time to expand your knowledge in these areas.

Questioning a Coach's Competence

Keep in mind that competence is largely a subjective perception that people have of you. One person might believe you are a genius and another a fool. Unfortunately, the perceptions others have of you often prevail over reality. If it is believed that a coach does not know how to devise a winning game plan nor make the proper adjustments within the game itself, he is often second-guessed by many including the fair-weather fans, partial parents, smug sportswriters, and the audacious arm-chair quarterbacks who fill the sports talk show radio waves. When you become a coach, everyone believes that they have a right to critique your every move.

At the youth sports level and often higher, parents are notorious for questioning the knowledge of their sons' and daughters' coaches, especially when, in their minds, little Tommy or Suzy is not getting the playing time he or she so obviously deserves. While certainly the parents' concern is warranted in some cases, parents' highly subjective feelings about their children's level of competence can skew their views of a coach's perceived competence. When the parents are continually telling their children that the coach doesn't know anything about the sport, it comes as no surprise that the children begin questioning the coach and become disrespectful. However, we believe that if you follow the suggestions in this book, you will have a much better chance of winning the respect of parents as well as your athletes.

In addition to parents, some coaches also openly question the competence of other coaches. In many sports you see a split between the high school coaches and the club sport coaches. Each of them questions the expertise level and motives of the other. Of course, this only confuses the athlete and often forces her to choose sides. Similarly, college and professional sport coaches are also having their credibility questioned and assailed by many including fans, owners, media, and sports agents. Just about everyone thinks that they have all of the answers. While most coaches can handle being scrutinized by outsiders, if your athletes themselves begin questioning your competence, your credibility and overall effectiveness are seriously jeopardized.

Lack of Playing Experience and Fitness Can Hurt

There are two potential barriers that can cause athletes to question your competence. The first is a coach's lack of playing experience, either at the level he coaches, or a lack of playing experience in the sport. Although it might seem unfair for athletes to judge their coach's competence by his playing experience or lack thereof, in reality, many judgments are unfortunately made this way. Athletes have a strong tendency to be skeptical of coaches who don't have a high level of playing experience. These coaches many times need to prove their competence even more so to their athletes. Although it can be more difficult initially, fortunately working harder and learning more can overcome a lack of playing experience. This will help you become a "guru" in a certain aspect of the game.

Kansas men's basketball coach Roy Williams is a good example of a coach who had minimal experience playing basketball at the college level. Williams played on the freshmen team at North Carolina but admitted that he wasn't talented enough to make the varsity. However, Williams had a passion to coach and diverted his focus from playing to coaching. He built his knowledge and philosophy while assisting Dean Smith and eventually got a chance to prove his competence as a coach at the University of Kansas.

Josh Pastner is a great example of another person who beat the odds. Pastner walked on to the University of Arizona's basketball team primarily because of his burning desire to be a coach. Pastner would have been a solid player in the intramural league, but at 5'11" he lacked the size and quickness to play at the Division I level. While his teammates gave him a hard time at first, they soon saw how passionate Pastner was about the game and how much he knew about it. Pastner spent hours helping his teammates develop by rebounding their shots, giving them pointers, and building their confidence. In a very short period of time, all of Arizona's players came to respect Pastner's knowledge and looked to him for guidance. Pastner's coaching ability actually became such a key component that coach Lute Olson even awarded Pastner with a full scholarship for the next three years. NBA point guard Mike Bibby still seeks Pastner's counsel.

Despite his modest playing ability, Pastner earned the respect of many elite players and coaches based on his passion, hard work, and knowledge of the game.

Thus, while your athletes might initially examine your playing experience in an effort to assess your credibility, it is not a requirement for being a credible coach. Oftentimes the best coaches weren't the best athletes. Because they didn't possess all of the physical gifts, they often had to develop other mental and tactical skills to gain an advantage as an athlete. It's these skills that become a tremendous asset when they move into coaching.

In today's world where first impressions are often based on appearance, coaches must be especially cognizant of the image they portray. A coach's fitness level and weight can initially help or hurt their perceived competence. Like it or not, athletes often view overweight and out of shape coaches as having less competence and credibility. They question why they should listen to you about being in shape when you yourself are winded after climbing a set of stairs. While you don't have to be an Iron Man triathlete to gain your athletes' respect, be conscious of your own physique and fitness level if you are looking to build and maintain your competence with your athletes.

Past Track Record of Success Can Help

Having a past track record of success goes a long way in enhancing your perceived competence. Coaches like Rick Pitino, Carolyn Peck, and Lou Holtz are automatically accorded a certain amount of respect because they have developed past champions. Also, if you have coached individual athletes who won all-conference and All-American honors, or who have earned a college scholarship or been drafted, this too can bolster your competence in the eyes of your athletes. Athletes will be more open to listening to you because you have taken others where they want to go.

How do you become more competent if you don't already have a past track record of success? Obviously your competence can be built through experience. However, few coaches have the time nor the job security to simply rely on the gradual process of gaining experience to build your competence. Therefore, credible coaches must invest the time to build their competence which brings us to our second major point.

Credible Coaches are Inquisitive and Innovative

"The last coach I had was not very innovative. She had us do the same things every year. We never really learned anything new."

High School Softball Player

Admit it; you love the kids who come early to practice as well as stay late to get some extra work and improve themselves. These athletes are never satisfied and know that there is always room for improvement. Coaches love athletes who are willing to dedicate extra time to developing their games.

Of course this same principle holds true for coaches. The highly credible coaches we interviewed, despite winning numerous championships and coach of the year honors, have an insatiable appetite to improve. No matter how successful and knowledgeable they might be, they are never satisfied that they know it all. These coaches realize the necessity to be lifelong students of the game. They are always open to new ideas, strategies, and equipment that might help them improve.

"You must be a student of the game and a lifelong student of the game. Even toward the end of your career, you're looking for the newest innovations and creations in your sport, and the newest message of teaching and programming your athletes."

Bill Walsh, Former San Francisco 49ers Coach

"Continual learning is a key to effective leadership... Because when you stop growing, you start to decay."

Mike Krzyzewski, Duke University Men's Basketball

Beware of the Comfort Zone

After years of coaching the same way, some coaches get locked into a comfort zone. They feel that they have found something that works and they stick to it. They lose their thirst for getting better. They stop going to coaches clinics for new ideas. They don't bother reading books or watching videos. And sooner or later, the game passes them by. Like Montgomery Wards and other once successful businesses that eventually become outdated and obsolete, we all know coaches who might have been successful in their time, but because they didn't keep up to date with the game, recruiting, or knowing how to relate to athletes, the game simply passed them by. It's really sad to see because these coaches merely wanted to maintain the status quo, while forgetting that coaches must change, grow, and improve with the times.

"I think some coaches will not adapt or adjust. They think this is the way we've been doing things for 15 years and this is what I am comfortable with. And that's what they're going to do. And as much as you want to take your team out of that comfort level to get better, you need to take yourself out of that comfort level to get better as well."

Gail Goestenkors, Duke University Women's Basketball

"Sometimes the most important listening you do is the listening that comes after you've reached the top, after you've gotten very good and could be susceptive to the idea that you know everything. Even though you're having a lot of success, you still have to be open. That's how you keep growing, keep competing, even after you've reached that high level, because there are a lot of people out there who can affect you and help you and teach you."

Dan Gable, Former University of Iowa Wrestling Coach

"When you think you have all the answers and you have it all figured out— that's when you are in trouble. You always have to be open for new ideas and be open to people's recommendations or suggestions."

Jerry Yeagley, Indiana University Men's Soccer

Since you are reading this book, you obviously believe in the importance of improving yourself and we commend you for it. Credible coaches tend to be ravenous readers. They love to read coaches' books in search of winning principles and new ideas. Not only do they read the autobiographies and biographies of coaches, they often explore other disciplines for new ideas they can incorporate. Credible coaches have been known to read books on a wide variety of topics including business, philosophy, psychology, military history, and sociology. In essence, they leave no page unturned if it has the potential to help them and their team.

"I am an avid, voracious reader and have always had difficulty not applying whatever I find in one book to whatever else I'm doing. So if it is the back of cereal boxes or psychology books, I'm always interested in how that applies to coaching," says former Nebraska volleyball coach and current coach advocate Terry Pettit.

Why do credible coaches spend so much time improving themselves and their programs? University of Arizona softball coach Mike Candrea believes that good coaches spend a great deal of time evaluating their teams. Coaches continually evaluate their players, their program, and themselves. In doing this, there inevitably will be areas that need to be improved. It is the coach's job then to be on the lookout for new and different ways to improve their weaknesses.

Credible coaches continually invest the time to build their understanding by doing whatever they can to find new ideas. They engage in continuous learning by attending clinics, watching videos, and reading books. Take a moment to assess how many clinics or professional development seminars you attended in the past few years. How many books have you read that relate to coaching or leading people? Have you developed and improved as much as you encourage your athletes to improve?

"You should learn as if you were going to live forever, and live as if you were going to die tomorrow... Always be learning, acquiring knowledge and wisdom for that long journey ahead. Know that when you are through learning, you are through."

John Wooden, Former UCLA Men's Basketball Coach

Credible Coaches are Human and Humble

"Coach isn't afraid to admit when he is wrong. He will flat out tell us when he let us down or made a mistake. That makes you respect a coach more than one who never admits he is wrong."

College Distance Runner

Perhaps one of the most interesting and inspiring things that we found in our interviews of credible coaches and their athletes is that they tend to be humble people who are not afraid to admit their mistakes.

Credible coaches realize that you can actually build your competence when you are willing to admit that you don't know it all. While this might seem like a paradox, you actually enhance your competence when you have the confidence to say you made a mistake or don't know the answer.

Why are credible coaches so willing to acknowledge their mistakes and shortcomings? This occurs largely because they have learned how to become secure with themselves. They know that they will make mistakes here and there and aren't afraid to admit them when they occur. This in turn builds their competence because the people around them respect them even more for being honest.

However, some coaches, especially when they are younger, are afraid of making mistakes and can't admit them when they occur. It is as if they must be perfect or people will see their weaknesses. In essence, coaches who are afraid to admit their mistakes or that they don't know everything tend to lack confidence because they are so unsure of themselves. So much of what young coaches do is to put up a front of competence and certainty when deep down inside they can't admit they are often scared and worried about being exposed. Therefore they tend to throw around their power and deny mistakes in an effort to protect themselves and their ego. In reality, if they were to admit they are human and make mistakes, they would actually gain the credibility they desire.

"A leader has to show that he's real, that he can make a mistake... When a leader makes a mistake and doesn't admit it, he is seen as arrogant or untrustworthy. And 'untrustworthy' is the last thing a leader wants to be... I've learned that to admit a mistake is not a weakness, it's a strength."
Mike Krzyzewski, Duke University Men's Basketball

"It is so important that the players understand that when I have messed up, I admit it. I think that helps build trust."
Mary Wise, University of Florida Volleyball

University of Nebraska softball coach Rhonda Revelle invested the time to build her competence early in her coaching career. After being a stand-out pitcher for the Huskers, Revelle eventually became the head coach of the team. While she knew pitching like the back of her hand, hitting was another story. Instead of trying to hide her lack of hitting knowledge, she willingly admitted her desire to learn and sought out University of Arizona softball coach Mike Candrea, who is considered one of the gurus of hitting. Revelle spent a lot of time talking with Candrea, asking questions, watching his videos, and traveling to Arizona to observe his practices. Over time,

Revelle built up her competence in hitting and has become a more complete and well-rounded coach.

Because credible coaches are able to acknowledge their shortcomings, they often will surround themselves with others who can compensate for any weaknesses they might have. They purposely recruit staff members who can complement their strengths and they aren't afraid to hire people who are more talented than they are in certain areas. Pat Summitt specifically hired assistant coach Mickie DeMoss away from Auburn because, in Summitt's words, "Mickie was better than I was" when it came to signing the nation's best players. By assembling a stellar staff who complemented her, Coach Summitt gave her program the edge it needed to consistently make it to the top.

It's Not Hard to Be Humble for Credible Coaches

Despite numerous wins, championships, and a wealth of personal successes, credible coaches are down to earth people who keep their sports and coaching careers in perspective. They understand that they have achieved a special level of success in their sports and have a certain amount of confidence in themselves because of it. However, they do not flaunt their success nor take it for granted. They realize that success is fleeting and that they must continually work to build their programs. They know how to handle the many temptations that surround success and are able to keep themselves on track and their priorities in order.

"Success can be a minefield, full of hidden obstacles and booby traps just waiting to trip you up. Success never comes sugar coated with guarantees of longevity. A few missteps, a few moments of letting down your guard—this is a poisonous pill that, if swallowed, can turn long-striven-for success into overnight failure."

Rick Pitino, University of Louisville Men's Basketball

"People with humility don't think less of themselves... They just think about themselves less."

Ken Blanchard & Norman Vincent Peale, Professional Speakers and Authors

As part of their humility, credible coaches have a deep respect for the game. They feel a strong indebtedness to the sports that have given them so much and are almost compelled to give back to it whenever they can.

Pat Summitt constantly does whatever she can to promote women's basketball—playing in outdoor basketball games, allowing cameras in her locker room, and wearing a microphone while she is coaching. She says, "I've always felt a responsibility to give back to this game because I could never do as much for this game as this game has done for me. Never! And I could coach until I was 100 years old and still not do it."

Questions for Reflection

- How would your athletes rate your competence with regard to the rules, mechanics, and strategy?
- How many clinics, seminars, or conferences have you attended in the last year?
- How many books, videos, and other resources have you used to improve yourself over the last year?
- How easy is it for you to admit when you are wrong?
- How do you handle success?

Chapter Eight Key Points

- To be considered competent you must have a thorough understanding of the rules, mechanics, and strategies of your sport.
- Your competence will be questioned by a variety of people including parents, athletic directors, media, and fellow coaches.
- Be aware of how your past playing experience and your physique can affect your perceived competence.
- Continually explore ways to get better by reading books and attending clinics and seminars.
- Have the courage to own up to your mistakes when they occur. Ironically, it helps you gain greater respect.
- Be confident on the inside yet humble on the outside.
- Keep your successes (and failures) in perspective.

MARY WISE

Head Volleyball Coach
University of Florida

Two-time National Coach of the Year

On Character

I think you have to understand yourself as a coach first instead of trying to be someone else. I think the sooner you figure out who you are, then you don't have to worry about all the other stuff.

I think there is a big difference between like and respect. Respect is more important. Respect has to be earned and we are constantly putting ourselves in a position where we earn each other's respect. The bonus is if we like each other. Then it's much easier to spend time with them. But liking is not more important than respect.

On Competence

I've been coaching for years and I still don't know all the answers. To keep it in the beginner's mind, that would be the best advice. To have a beginner's mind is what we teach our athletes, but you as a coach have to have that as well.

On Confidence Building

As a coach you must understand the uniqueness of each individual. What buttons can you push? When can you push them? When do you have to back off? Each player responds very differently. We try to learn what makes them happy, what motivates them, and what they like to do.

Good coaches put their players in a position to succeed.

When we have lost, I have taken the blame. If we're not prepared, that is my fault. If practice is bad, that is the coach's fault. If it was poorly designed, poorly run, poorly communicated, then I look here first.

On Caring

It's not about the coach; it's not about me. It's about these players and where they come from and what makes them respond.

On Consistency

When you lose and you're mad, the worst mistake we do as coaches is remove ourselves. If the team is losing, that's when they need coaching the most, and yet coaches will back away. You can see coaches sitting on the bench that they have checked out. It's real easy when you're winning to be close to the court and cheerleading, but that's not when they need it. They need it when you're losing.

Jerry Yeagley, Former Head Men's Soccer Coach, Indiana University

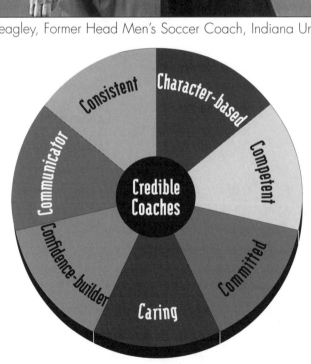

CHAPTER NINE

Credible Coaches Are COMMITTED

Having A Passion For Coaching

"There are only two options regarding commitment. You're either IN or you're OUT. There's no such thing as life in-between."

Pat Riley, Miami Heat

Commitment is such a buzzword in sport. There is hardly a day that passes without coaches or athletes discussing commitment and its impact on their success. A strong commitment is one of the most important factors in success. Conversely, a lack of commitment is often the reason cited for failure.

There is little doubt that commitment is an essential component of great leadership. Take a moment to think about three people you would consider to be great leaders. What would you say about their level of commitment to their chosen profession or cause? You most likely would include the following attributes in your description of these people. They are fully invested in whatever they are doing. They have a vision of greatness and a well thought out plan to accomplish their goals. They have a burning passion for their vision and are able to get other people to buy into their vision. And finally, these people are willing to work hard and long and persevere through difficult times to make sure their vision becomes a reality.

Not surprisingly, we have found that your athletes look for the same traits in you as their coach. They want you to be fully committed to them and the sport you coach. They want you to be unafraid to dream and able to share your passion for a clear vision with them. They want you to be confident about building and maintaining a winning program. And they want you to be willing to work harder than anyone else to take them to "the promise land."

Are you a committed coach? Would your athletes say they respect you for your dedication to them and your sport? As we further discuss commitment, we would encourage you to carefully examine your current situation and determine if your athletes would characterize you as a credible coach in the area of commitment.

"You must be absolutely committed to your athletes. It is important that they know you will fight to get the best of everything for them."

Jolene Nagel, Duke University Women's Volleyball

"There are three things you need to be committed to as a coach—people, your sport, and your profession. If you don't have a passion for those three things, you will not be an effective coach."

Bob Jenkins, Former National High School Track Coach of the Year

Your Commitment Influences Your Athletes' Commitment

Before we try to sell you on the importance of being a committed coach, it is necessary to address a frustration that coaches often mention to us. It has to do with the perceived lack of commitment on the part of their athletes. Many coaches have said that their level of commitment is much higher than that of their athletes and it is very frustrating and causes them to enjoy coaching much less. The reality is that some athletes will never match their coach's level of commitment.

While coaches at all levels are faced with commitment issues of their athletes, those of you coaching at the college level contend with a special case of potential contentment on the part of some of your athletes. Most of your athletes have been dedicated to their particular sport since they were very young. Some athletes continue with that commitment because they either want to compete at the next level or they want to coach their sport someday. The athletes in these two groups tend to be very committed to improving and doing what it takes to accomplish their ultimate goals. There is another group of athletes who have also been dedicated to their sport for a long time, but their ultimate goal has been to compete at the college level. Once they have reached this goal, some of them find it hard to continue with that same level of commitment.

For those of you who are frustrated because of a lack of commitment on the part of your athletes, we would encourage you to incorporate the suggestions we have provided throughout this book into your every day coaching. If you are able to do this, those less committed athletes will be more likely to develop a strong commitment to you and their sport. It has been said that a team takes on the personality of its coach. Nowhere is that more relevant than when it comes to a coach's commitment. If you are committed to your athletes and your sport, they will be more likely to be committed, which in turn will alleviate some of your frustrations and help you enjoy what you are doing much more. It is a cycle that often begins with you and the environment that you create as the coach. That said, the following suggestions are provided to help you demonstrate a strong commitment to your athletes and your sport.

Successful Vision

"How can we believe in ourselves if coach doesn't believe in us? It seems like she just goes through the motions and has no real vision of what she wants us to do."

College Women's Volleyball Player

Being a committed coach begins with having a vision of success for your athletes and your program. Most great accomplishments begin with a dream of what might be possible. Regardless of what kind of team they have or inherit, credible coaches spend a significant amount of time thinking about the possibilities for their athletes and teams. It's pretty easy to have visions of greatness when you have a talented team. The real challenge is envisioning a bright future when you have a losing team or takeover a poor program. It is this vision of a better future that will keep both you and your athletes positive and optimistic as your team makes the climb to the top.

When thinking about your vision for individuals or your team, we would encourage you to dream about the possibilities if everything fell into place the way you think it could (i.e. if everyone stayed relatively healthy, you win the competitions you are supposed to win and you surprise a few opponents you are not supposed to defeat). What could your team accomplish? Sometimes having a .500 or greater record would be considered a major success for a season depending on what kind of team you have.

Once you have established the ideal outcome, you need to formulate a realistic and workable plan for your team to follow. You must break your vision down into practical steps that your players can take on a daily basis. You have got to be convinced that your plan will work because ultimately you will be selling it to your athletes.

"My first act of being named head coach of the Bulls was to formulate a vision for the team. I started by creating a vivid picture in my mind of what the team could become. I had to take into account not only what I wanted to achieve, but how I was going to get there."

Phil Jackson, Los Angeles Lakers

Passion

"Coach has passion. No doubt about that. You can see that everyday we come to practice. He expects that same level of enthusiasm from us."

High School Baseball Player

Once you have developed a vision, it is necessary to let others see the passion you have for it. You have to be sold on it and be able to sell others in your program on it. One way to do that is to live your vision every day. Walk it and talk it with passion. To begin to assess your degree of passion, take a few minutes to honestly answer the following questions: Do you still have a passion for coaching like you did when you first started? Do you get excited to go to practice every day? Do you still feel that little bit of nervousness before competitions? Do you look forward to the start of a new season each year? If the answer to any of these questions is no, you will have a hard time conveying optimism and enthusiasm to your athletes. This lack of perceived passion can affect your attitude, which in turn has a profound effect on the athletes you coach. There is an old saying, "Attitudes are contagious, make yours worth catching." Credible coaches have attitudes worth catching because they have a passion for their sport and coaching. They love what they do and seem to be totally invested in what they are doing. Credible coaches are so passionate about coaching they almost feel as if coaching chose them, rather than them choosing to be coaches.

"You can't lead others to places you don't want to go yourself."
James Kouzes and Barry Posner, Authors of *Encouraging the Heart*

"If you aren't fired with enthusiasm, you will be fired with enthusiasm."
Vince Lombardi, Former Green Bay Packers Coach

For the Love or the Money?

The way sport is in our society, some coaches are paid millions of dollars, some are paid very little, and some are paid nothing. Those coaches who aren't volunteers and who truly have a passion for coaching would coach even if they were being paid very little. Some would coach even if they were being paid nothing. How about you? Would you do what you do if you were paid significantly less than what you are currently being paid? Those of you who are being paid might balk at this idea and probably wouldn't coach— at least at your current level. Did you get into coaching so that you could make a lot of money? Most of you probably got into coaching because you loved your sport and you enjoyed teaching athletes to better themselves. Somewhere along the line, some coaches lose sight of why they began coaching in the first place. Certain groups of coaches will argue that they have lost their love for coaching because kids are different today and it takes much more effort to coach them. For other coaches, it becomes more about the money. This often happens when coaches are in the early stages of their careers and interested in moving up the career ladder.

At one college program, the athletes have said that their coach seems to only be in it for the money. Based on some of his comments and his lack of interaction with his athletes, they feel this coach continues to coach because of the money that can be made from summer camps. These athletes have very little respect for this coach and find it hard to be committed to him and the program. In fact, they have begun to negatively recruit for this coach. In other words, they tell potential recruits they probably don't want to come to this particular school to play. But if they do come, they need to be prepared to play for a coach who lacks passion and is only concerned with making money. Whether or not these perceptions are correct, the idea that these athletes view their coach in this way severely diminishes his credibility.

So, can you honestly say that you have a passion for your sport and the athletes you coach? If so, can your athletes and those around you sense that passion? If not, are you willing to do what it takes to rediscover that passion?

Hard Working

"It's hard to imagine that anyone outworks her. She is one of those coaches that when she asks you to play hard, you know she isn't asking anything of you that she wouldn't do herself if she was playing. Her work ethic is awesome."

College Women's Basketball Player

If there is one area that most athletes say their coaches lead by positive example, it is in the area of hard work. Most coaches that we have worked with or observed are more than willing to work hard and long hours to help their athletes be successful. Many coaches are willing to work on their fields and courts or do whatever it takes to make sure their athletes have the best possible facilities on which to compete. Spending countless hours viewing film and scouting opponents is a common occurrence in most programs.

This love for hard work usually began at an early age. Many of the credible coaches we interviewed were raised by proud and hard working parents who earned a modest income. The coaches learned the value of hard work by watching their parents work long hours to support their family.

While you are very likely a committed coach, we would use an even stronger word to describe the highly successful coaches we interviewed—compelled. These coaches were totally invested in building and maintaining winning programs. Regardless of their budget, previous records, or past recruits, these coaches would not rest until they put their programs into a position to be successful.

Tennessee women's basketball coach Pat Summitt believes that so few coaches could match her compelling work ethic that she willingly revealed the inner workings of her program in her book *Reach for the Summit*. Coach Summitt writes, "A lot of people said to me when I set out to write this book, 'Aren't you afraid of giving away all your secrets?' The answer is just plain no. I could throw open the door of our locker room and show you all the inner workings of our program, and you still wouldn't beat us, if you weren't willing to outwork us." She reiterated her thoughts in our interview with her. "There's nobody in this profession who will outwork me. Now you can think that you're going to do it and that's fine. They can work as hard as me, but they're not going to outwork me."

"I ask for the same dedication of extra work and high focus from the players as I do from myself."

Phil Jackson, Los Angeles Lakers

"I've been fortunate that my commitment almost demands that the players have the same type of commitment. And I've had players in the past say 'Coach works so hard it sort of embarrasses us if we don't work that hard.' I think the commitment I give them sort of asks for them to give that back without me saying anything."

Roy Williams, University of North Carolina Men's Basketball

Competitive

"My coach is the most competitive person I know. She hates to lose and I really like that. I wouldn't want to play for someone who didn't have that desire to win. What would be the use of working so hard?"

College Volleyball Player

Some of you reading this book might be thinking that we are trying to create a bunch of "soft" coaches who aren't competitive. Nothing could be further from the truth. Spend just a few minutes with Mike Krzyzewski, Pat Summitt, or Mike Candrea and you will soon discover that they are anything but "soft." Many of the athletes we spoke with indicated that it was very important for their coach to be a competitor—someone who liked to win. The credible coaches we have worked with are among the most competitive people we have ever met. They want to win and "have that fire in their bellies" or the "killer instinct" to be successful. They enjoy competing and winning. Underneath the public exterior is a "roaring lion" willing to do whatever it takes within the letter and spirit of the rules to win. Credible coaches are able to ward off complacency and contentment after big wins. They don't rest on their laurels because they know the next competition is the most important one.

Are you as competitive as you have always been? Do you still have that drive to excel as a coach? Just as it is with passion, your athletes will catch whatever attitude you model. If you are competitive, you will be more likely to have competitive athletes.

Maintaining a Healthy Balance

Because you are reading this book, you are probably a coach who is committed to working hard to build and maintain a successful program. In our discussion of commitment, we have said you need to be a visionary, have passion, and be extremely hard working and competitive. If you possess these characteristics, you will most likely have the respect of your athletes. The problem with these attributes is that an overabundance of them can lead to an early entrance into the "spent" stage of coaching as well as strained relationships with family, friends, and children. Therefore, it is important to have a strong commitment to your athletes and your sport. But, it is also important to have a balance in your life. You should have passion with perspective.

The way you have a healthy balance and avoid becoming stale is to "ride that fine line" between commitment and obsession. Your sport must be "a priority" for you to earn the respect of your athletes. However, it should not be "the priority" in your life. Joe Torre, the manager of the New York Yankees, said he spent way too much of his time early in his career focusing on himself and not his family. Now he realizes the importance of having a healthier balance between baseball and his family. He sacrificed having a close relationship with his children because he was so focused and obsessed with himself and advancing his career.

"Winning a football game isn't the end of all things. It's got a priority, but it's not number one in my life. This creates for me a certain amount of calmness, even though I'm human enough to suffer when we lose."

Tom Landry, Former Dallas Cowboys Coach

Keep Your Priorities in Order

If you take commitment to your athletes and your sport to the extreme, you can neglect the most important people in your life—your family and friends. University of Arizona softball coach Mike Candrea admits that he was too involved in the game early on in his career. Because he was so focused on taking his program to a championship level, he missed out on a lot of quality time with his wife Sue, and children Mikel and Michelle when they were young. Coach Candrea advises, "Knowing that I haven't been able to spend the kind of time with my own kids that I have with other kids is a struggle for me. A huge development in my life was becoming more aware of the things that are really important. You need to really be careful that you don't throw away everything that is really important to you when you are trying to win the big game. Winning the big game is not going to change your life all that much but if you lose your family, it certainly will. There is going to be a day when I am going to walk away from this game and I am going to have one thing left, and that is my family."

Coach Candrea continually emphasizes the need for balance in life with himself, his players, and with other coaches when he speaks at clinics. He says, "All coaches need to keep the game in perspective. If you can maintain a balance in your life you're going to survive longer in the profession and you're going to be happier. And if you are happier you are going to be a better coach. I get more compliments when I speak about balance in life than I do about the technical parts of the game."

Are You a Credible Spouse, Parent, and Friend?

While hopefully you rated yourself as a coach on the Seven Secrets of Successful Coaches, we strongly encourage you to rate yourself on the same seven characteristics as a spouse, friend, and/or parent. For those of you who are married, are you spending enough quality time with your spouse? Are you missing out on many of the things your children are experiencing as they grow because you are seldom home? What would your immediate family say about you and your relationship with them? Would your spouse say that you always put your relationship with him/her before anything else in this world? Would he/she say you take the time to ask about his/her life rather than always talking about your life and career? Would your children say that they know you love them because you tell them on a regular basis? Would your children say that you are there for them when they need you most? How about those you consider to be your friends? Would they say that you are a good friend and enjoyable to be around whether your team wins or loses?

It seems as though we are saying you have to be all things to all people. The reality is that coaching is a very time and energy consuming profession as many of you already know. To be a credible coach, you must be all of the things we have mentioned. But in this drive for earning and maintaining the respect of your athletes and colleagues, you cannot forget to have a balance. In the end, the people who are most important to you will remember you for the relationships you have with them.

Balance Means Mentally Leaving Coaching Behind

To have balance in your life you must be able to make the transition from being a coach to playing the other roles you have in your life. Being able to "leave coaching behind" and focus your energies and attention on the roles you play away from your sport is essential for a healthy balance. Here are a few suggestions to help you maintain a healthy balance between your role as a coach and those roles you play outside of your sport.

1. Be efficient with your time at the office and around your team. You might make a list of the important things you need to accomplish each day and make those the priority. When it is time to leave, make a list of the things you will do the next day. If you manage your time well and have a plan of attack for the following day, you will feel much better about going home.

2. Place something in your car as a reminder of where you are going. You can have a picture of your family on your dashboard or a little sticker on your rearview mirror to help you remember where you are going and the roles you need to begin to play.

3. Make it a point to ask others in your family or your friends about their day and what is happening in their lives. Coaches tend to be selfish and only want to talk about their days.

4. Be consistent in your mood whether or not your team wins or loses. We have heard families tell of how they have to "walk on eggshells" around the coach in their family for several hours or even days after a loss. They don't know what to expect from this person. This can't be healthy for family relationships.

5. Make time to do things with your family. There is no question this is easier during the off-season. But, doing things as a family when

you are fully invested in what is happening, will go a long way to show your family members they are as important as your athletic team. Nebraska football coach Tom Osborne would specifically set aside Wednesday nights as "Date Night" so that he and his wife could spend some quality time together on a regular basis during the hectic season. Just as you schedule and plan practices, you also should schedule some quality time to spend with your spouse, children, and friends.

We hope we have caused you to reflect on your level of commitment to your athletes, your program and the people in your personal life. Coaching is a very demanding profession. To be successful, you must have a vision, a passion for that vision, and be willing to work very hard. And you must do all of this while not neglecting your life away from the sport. The good news is that with a concerted effort on your part, you can strike a healthy balance and enjoy all aspects of your life.

Questions for Reflection

- How committed are you?
- What kind of vision have you created for your team?
- Are you coaching for the love of the game?
- How competitive are you?
- Are you a credible spouse, parent, and/or friend?
- Can you let go of coaching when it is time to play other roles in your life?

Chapter Nine Key Points

- Make a renewed commitment to your athletes and your sport.
- Create a great vision for your team.
- Put in the time necessary to help them realize that vision.
- Allow your passion to show in everything you do.
- Maintain a healthy balance in your life so that you will have the energy and resiliency it takes to be effective throughout your career.

JERRY YEAGLEY

Former Head Men's Soccer Coach, Indiana University

Six-time National Champions

Five-time National Coach of the Year

United States Soccer Federation
    Hall of Fame

On Character

Being honest and fair is very important. Kids will see through you if you try to set different standards for different people. You have to be totally honest and you have to be the role model. If you don't, your players won't respect you.

On Competence

I have learned things from youth coaches and high school coaches that I have incorporated into our system. I'm always trying to find if there is a better way.

On Commitment

I would like to be remembered by my players as someone who was passionate for the game—someone who had a burning desire to achieve. But who had the well being of the individual players first and someone who deeply cared about each and every player on the team.

On Caring

I'm a very hands on coach; very much a friend to my players. They laugh at me, I laugh at them. I have a way of joking around with them, yet when it is time for business and seriousness, I can make that transition. I wouldn't be a good 'dictator' coach because I like to be close to my players.

We have a very close alumni group. We have constant communication with them. We have get-togethers and I stay very close with the alums and they are very, very important in our recruiting. So I think that has been a big part of our success as well—and a big part of my personal enjoyment and reward of coaching.

On Consistency

As coaches we need to explain and be more sensitive to the student-athletes' needs. I try very hard to let my players know why we're doing certain things. I encourage them to ask and be inquisitive.

If you treat everyone the same you're going lose some because not everyone responds to the same motivation. You have to find out how to get through to them and get the most out of them. That's the real challenge and the interesting part of coaching, the thing that really stokes me and gets me going.

Roy Williams, Head Men's Basketball Coach, University of North Carolina

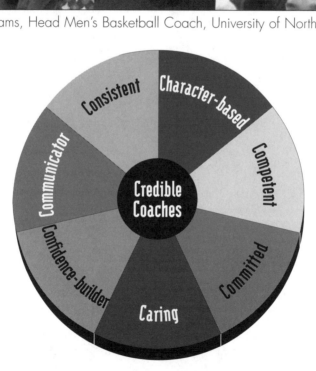

CHAPTER TEN

Credible Coaches Are CARING

People Don't Care How Much You Know Until They Know How Much You Care

"I know if somebody really cares about me and is really fighting for me, I'll go through a wall for them. The same works in reverse. If somebody knows you don't care about him and aren't really fighting for him, then he won't go through the wall for you."

Mike Shanahan, Denver Broncos

We'd like to begin this chapter with a little quiz that was sent to us by Wes Worrell, a credible coach at Bishop Kelly High School in Boise, Idaho.

1. Name the NCAA Final Four teams for men's or women's basketball over the last three years:
2. Name the last three Heisman trophy winners:
3. Name the last three National Player of the Year winners for college softball:
4. Name the three wealthiest people in the world:
5. Name three people who have won the Nobel Peace Prize or the Pulitzer Prize:

How did you do? If you are like most people, you are lucky if you were able to get more than one or two of these questions correct. While you may not have answered many of these questions correctly, obviously the people who achieved these special accomplishments have a great deal of talent. However, even though these people are the best of the best, eventually the applause dies down, the awards tarnish, and their achievements are forgotten (or never known by many). The point is, very few of us remember the past successes of others.

Here's a make up exam for you—see how you do on this one...

1. Name three people who have helped bring out the best in you:
2. Name three people who have made you feel appreciated and special:
3. Name three people who you enjoy spending time with:
4. Name three people who have helped you through a difficult time:
5. Name three people who you really trust:

Was this a bit easier for you? Why—what's the lesson here? The people who make the biggest difference in our lives are not necessarily the ones with the best credentials, the most money, or the greatest success. The people who have the biggest impact on us are the ones who truly care about us.

Here's what this means to you as a coach: At the end of your career very few of your athletes will know your exact win-loss record. They will forget the scores of the majority of competitions they played in. They won't be able to recall how many conference titles you had or how many Coach of the Year awards you might have won. However, they will most certainly know whether or not you truly cared about them.

"I think that when kids leave college they remember number one, their friendships, and number two, their relationship with their coach. They don't remember the wins. Obviously they'll remember some of them. Overall, that's not what they'll remember. And they don't remember, 'Oh, she was good at X's and O's.' They remember, 'Did she care about me or did she not.'"

Gail Goestenkors, Duke University Women's Basketball

Former North Carolina men's basketball Coach Dean Smith is the perfect example of a coach who left a tremendous legacy both on and off the court. In 1997, Smith's Tar Heels had a second round NCAA tournament game against Colorado in Winston-Salem, North Carolina. A win would not only advance the Tar Heels to the Sweet Sixteen but also push Smith past Adolph Rupp as the winningest men's basketball coach of all-time. Many of Smith's former players stopped whatever they were doing and flew to Winston-Salem to be at the game. As usual, Smith's team won the game for his 877th career victory. As Smith went out of the tunnel leading back to the locker room after the game, there were dozens of his former players lining the sides to congratulate him. Coach Smith was overcome with emotion realizing that so many of his former players would drop everything to be there. With tears in his eyes, he shook the hand of every former player who had come out of respect for their beloved coach and thanked them for all that they had done for him.

"It's not just the great ones I remember. I remember everyone of them, and not just as ballplayers. I remember the ones who didn't play much but nevertheless helped our teams in countless ways, as well as those who went on to win individual honors..."

Dean Smith, Former University of North Carolina Men's Basketball Coach

What it Means to Care

If you truly want to be a credible coach you must like working with people. After all, coaches are really in the people development business. Not only must you like people, but more importantly, you must also be willing to love them. Love might seem to be a strange and uncomfortable concept for some coaches but it's true. Credible coaches genuinely care about the people they coach. They learn to love their athletes even though they might not always like them.

"I've never had a player I didn't love. I've had many I didn't like and didn't respect. But I loved them just the same."

Amos Alonzo Stagg, Former University of Chicago Football Coach

"At Nebraska, our coaching staff was encouraged to genuinely love and care about their players. In other words, each of them was expected to demonstrate an unconditional positive regard toward the player's total well-being."

Tom Osborne, Former University of Nebraska Football Coach

Don't all coaches care about their athletes? The answer in our opinion is yes and no. Yes we believe that all coaches care about their athletes to some degree. In fact, the vast majority of coaches we know care deeply about their players. However, too many times coaches are reluctant to fully show their athletes how much they care about them. Sometimes coaches feel they can't show their athletes that they care because it might jeopardize their sense of control or power. Therefore they intentionally keep their distance from their players-guarding their emotions and never really opening up to them. However we feel the risks are much greater for you and your athletes when you don't show your athletes that you care. If you aren't willing to share your heart with your athletes, they will be very unlikely to share their hearts with you. But, when you coach from your heart, you capture the power of their hearts.

We have seen numerous situations where coaches got consumed with winning and did not seem to care about their athletes. For example, when coaches spend little time and attention on their substitutes and treat them like second class citizens, athletes question how much they care about them. When coaches force players to play despite serious injuries, athletes question how much they care about them. When coaches psychologically torture and belittle their players, athletes wonder how much they care about them. When college coaches push athletes into easy and convenient majors just for the sake of keeping them eligible or not missing practice time, athletes question how much they care about them. When coaches rarely or never keep in touch with their former players after their playing careers are over, athletes wonder how much they care about them. When coaches blatantly use their teams as stepping stones to more prestigious and higher paying jobs, athletes wonder how much they care about them.

An Overview of Caring

Through our interviews and work with highly credible coaches we found three primary areas that emerged in terms of the caring factor. First, credible coaches take a holistic approach to their athletes' development. They want what is best for them not just in sport but also in the game of life. Secondly, credible coaches adopt the servant philosophy of leadership. This means that coaches willingly sacrifice their own time and glory because they want to help their people succeed. They make their athletes' success the overall priority, rather than their own. Finally, credible coaches don't stop caring about their athletes just because they finish their eligibility, get injured, or leave the team. The caring for the person continues far beyond their usefulness as an athlete, often throughout the rest of the person's life.

Caring Must Come from the Heart

Although we are going to describe some steps to help you come across as being a more caring and compassionate coach, ultimately your caring must be genuine and come from the heart. We remind you once again of the title of Coach Krzyzewski's book *Leading with the Heart*. Caring for your athletes must be part of your overall philosophy rather than just a set of prescribed actions. Odds are you want to make a real difference in people's lives and leave a lasting legacy with those you coach. Let this core value be your guide as you look to express your underlying compassion to your athletes. It may feel like a risk, but the rewards, both professionally and personally, are well worth it!

Caring for the Total Person, Not Just the Athlete

"Coach is always asking us about school and life. He really makes you feel like he cares about you as a person."

College Football Player

Credible coaches genuinely care about all aspects of their athletes' lives. They are interested in each person's overall success, not just what the athlete can do for them on the court or field. They take the time to get to know their athletes on a personal level, being interested in their family, friends, faith, and future goals.

North Carolina men's basketball coach Roy Williams believes that showing your athletes that you care about their overall well being is extremely important. He says, "Players do need to feel that we care. I think they need to feel even more so that we care for them off the court. On the court they know we're trying to win. They understand that. But off the court I want the kids to understand how important it is that I care about what they do academically; caring that they are on progress toward a degree. I want them to understand that basketball games are important. But each and every day I'm trying to get them prepared for life, because so few are really going to go ahead and play the game for a living."

"One of the finest things a player could say about me after he left the team was that I cared every bit about him as an individual as I care about him as an athlete. There was a great deal of love involved in my coaching."
John Wooden, Former UCLA Men's Basketball Coach

"You have to make sure that your players understand that you care about them. That includes what they're doing away from the rink—their families and the things that are going on in their lives that sort of are outside the sphere of sport."
Tom Renney, Director of Player Personnel, New York Rangers

How Much Do You Know About Your Athletes as People? Exercise

Take a moment to assess how much you know about your athletes' lives away from sport.

- Do you know what each of your athletes want to do with their lives when their athletic careers are over?
- What are their interests and hobbies outside of sport?
- Do you know who their best friends are?
- What kind of relationship do they have with their parents?
- Do they have any brothers or sisters?
- Are they currently dating anyone?
- Do you know their birthdays?

These are all important questions to your athletes. If they are important to them, then they also should be important to you.

Each of these outside variables impacts your players' mood, focus, confidence, and commitment. It is in everyone's best interest that you have a sufficient knowledge about what is going on with each of your athletes outside of sport. Knowing that a player's grandfather was just diagnosed with cancer might help you to be a little more understanding when he is struggling at practice. Or congratulating one of your athletes because she has just become an aunt for the first time is a great way to make her day. Cutting out an article you saw in the paper that relates to your athlete's career plans shows him that you are interested.

The best way to get to know your athletes better is to invest the time to chat with them. Ask them how their families are doing or how their classes are going. Too many coaches have a tendency to only talk with their athletes about their sport. Instead, invest the time to get to know them as people.

When you do talk with them about things outside of sport, be sure that you are not putting them on the "hot seat" and grilling them. You must fight the tendency to want to talk about their sport right away. We know of a coach whose athletes steer clear of the office despite his "open door policy." If they must stop by the office, the athletes quietly ask the secretary if the coach is in. If she nods in agreement, they escape quickly, hoping to leave unnoticed. This is because whenever the coach sees his players he unwittingly corrals them and interrogates them about themselves and the team like a merciless detective forcing a confession. It is no wonder they avoid him like the plague and dread talking with him.

"When my players come into my office I try not to always go right to basketball. I first ask them, 'How's school going? What's going on?' I don't want them to see my office as a prison. They want to sit in the chair to relax and not feel like they're always in the hot seat. Instead I talk with them about their settings off of the court."

Pat Summitt, University of Tennessee Women's Basketball

Trust Takes Time

One of the comments we heard from athletes is that some coaches wanted to know too much about them and tried to get too involved in their personal lives. As former Nebraska volleyball coach Terry Pettit cautions, "Athletes need to know that you care about them but there is also a fine line. The fine line is that if you go over the line, the athletes feel that you are invading their life—that you are too concerned about who they are dating or what they are doing socially. They need their space." Keep in mind that you can't know everything nor should you want to.

You must remember to let the athlete take the lead in what he or she wants to reveal to you. Trust is a process that takes time so you must be patient. You can't expect your athletes to just open up and reveal their deepest, darkest secrets to you right away.

Building trust with athletes is a lot like feeding a wild animal some food out of your hand. At first, both you and the animal proceed with great caution because you are very weary of being harmed. However, if you reach out your hand with the food and be patient, the animal will begin inching toward you but still fearful that your motives may be less than pure. Eventually, if you remain poised and patient, the animal may accept what you have to offer. Over time, provided that you maintain your helpful intent and posture, the animal will become more and more trusting and comfortable with you—just like the athlete.

The key to gaining your athletes' trust is to create an open, interested, nonjudgmental, and supportive environment. Some may open up to you very quickly while others, because of their nature or personality, may take months or even years. Keep in mind that you can't force them to open up and you don't need to know absolutely everything about your athletes. However, you do need to show them that you are sincerely interested in them as people.

Six Ideas for Showing Your Athletes That You Care

1. Have people over for dinner at your house.
Duke men's basketball coach Mike Krzyzewski makes a point of having each of his players over to his house for dinner. During this time he casually checks in with them and takes the time to chat.

2. Meet with people regularly to talk.
Some coaches schedule regular meetings with their athletes to check in with them. Again, remember to talk to them as people, not just as athletes.

3. Have informal chats.
Hang out with your athletes before practice, in the locker room, in your

office. Just being around them gives you opportunities to get to know them a lot better.

4. Acknowledge and appreciate the outside stuff.
Take an interest in the other hobbies and events in your athletes' lives. Acknowledge them in front of the team for getting an "A" on a test.

5. Spend time with injured athletes.
You send a clear message that you really don't care about your athletes as people if you aren't willing to spend time with them when they are injured. Take the time to ask injured athletes how their rehabilitation is progressing and let them know that they are still an integral part of the team.

6. Visit with your athletes' parents/families.
When taking over new programs, some coaches have traveled around the country to sit down with each of their current athletes' parents in their homes. The travel was exhausting, but these coaches indicate it was one of the best things they have ever done. It gave them a chance to get to know both their athletes and their parents much better. Plus it showed how much these coaches cared since they were willing to travel long distances to spend time with them in their homes. While visiting all of your athletes might be a heavy financial and time-consuming burden for some of you, you could easily invest the time to call each of your players' parents.

Credible Coaches are Selfless, Servant Leaders

"He is the most selfless coach I know. He is always looking out for his players and tries to put us first. I don't think I have ever heard him take credit for a win. But, I have heard him take the blame when we lost. It really isn't about him."

College Men's Lacrosse Player

Let's look at another Dean Smith story to introduce this next concept. Going into the 1982 NCAA tournament, Coach Smith had led his team to six Final Fours. While this alone seems to be an amazing accomplishment, Coach Smith was criticized by many for not being able to win the Big One.

Smith's talented Tar Heels advanced through the tournament and eventually beat an excellent Georgetown team for the title. Upon returning to Chapel Hill, the University held a huge celebration for the team at their football stadium. However, despite a chance to get vindication over all of his naysayers, Smith opted to skip the victory celebration and instead went for a walk in a park with his daughter Kristen. Smith writes in his book *A Coach's Life*, "I didn't go, nor would I ever go to one. I felt those things should be for players, not for coaches." While some coaches seek the spotlight during times of success, Coach Smith wanted the focus to be on his players instead of himself.

Credible coaches are selfless. Their focus is to elevate others instead of themselves; they look to create heroes instead of be heroes. They willingly make sacrifices of their own time and glory in an effort to build others' careers instead of their own. In essence, credible coaches practice what many now call "servant leadership," a term first coined by author Robert Greenleaf in his book *Servant Leadership*. Using the life of Jesus as a model, Greenleaf found that the best leaders looked to serve their followers instead of having their followers serve them. This concept holds true for coaches. To paraphrase a famous saying by former President John Kennedy, "Ask not what your athletes can do for you, ask instead, What can you do for your athletes?"

"When I viewed myself as a servant of the other coaches and the players, things went better for our team and for me personally. This did not mean that I was any less demanding... It did mean however, that I was there to do whatever I could to help them accomplish team objectives and mature into better people."

Tom Osborne, Former University of Nebraska Football Coach

Make Your Players the Priority

Take a moment and consider, "Who is this really all about?" Whose success is the highest priority—yours or your athletes? If it's all about you—your career, your record, your reputation—your athletes will catch on very quickly. They will likely feel used and come to resent you. In some instances, we have seen athletes go so far as sabotaging their own success in an effort to keep their coaches from succeeding.

However, when your athletes feel like they are the priority, that it's about their success and not your own, they will readily give you their best effort. When you are willing to give so much of yourself to them, you will find that you will get even more in return. Your athletes will appreciate your selflessness and extend you their devotion and loyalty for a lifetime.

How do you show your athletes that they are the priority? As in life, it's not always the big things you do but the countless little things that truly make a difference. Dean Smith had a special phone line that was solely dedicated to his family and his players. Also, legend has it that Coach Smith once kicked out the chancellor of the University when one of his players wanted to talk. Despite the chancellor's rank, Smith's players knew that they were the priority.

"I think one of my strong suits as a manager is that I make the players understand that I do care about what's going on in their lives, not necessarily what's going on in the field."

Joe Torre, New York Yankees

"To be a truly great leader you must give of yourself. You can't be selfish. You must convey a vision of partnership, that you not only care about the people who work for you, but that it's important they're successful, too. It can't just be about you, your career, your success."

Rick Pitino, University of Louisville Men's Basketball

Mike Pressler, the men's lacrosse coach at Duke calls it "egoless" coaching. He feels it has to be about his players rather than himself. He always tries to make it a point to emphasize that it is the athletes who play the game. He has never made a last second shot or played great defense to stop someone from scoring. His players are the ones who play the game and they are the ones who should get the credit. Coach Pressler also allows his captains to sit in first class rather than the coaches when they are able to bump people up on trips. His players are always in front of the coaches in the line to eat. These little acts show his athletes that they are the priority on this team.

How Close are You with Your Athletes?

Obviously, the emphasis of this chapter focuses on the importance of developing compassionate and close connections with your athletes that go beyond the superficial coach-athlete relationship. When you get to know your athletes well and they feel you truly care about them as people, they will be much more willing to spill their guts for you. If your athletes see you as being detached and aloof, they may still work hard and execute, but seldom will they be motivated to kick it into a higher gear for you and realize their full potential.

Because she was so young when she got her first head coaching job, Duke women's basketball coach Gail Goestenkors initially tried not to get too close to her players. "In my first couple of years here I was not as comfortable with myself and I think part of that was it was my first head coaching job. I was the youngest coach in the conference so I wanted the players to know that there was a line. And sometimes, I think in retrospect, it was too big a line—a big gap—because I didn't want them to become too comfortable with me. So I think I've grown into feeling comfortable with who I am and my coaching abilities. It's allowed me to get close to my team which I think has benefited both of us."

"The best way to motivate your players is to try to get to know them as people and to care about them as people. And then, just maybe then, they'll open up and you can get in on a deeper level."
Rhonda Revelle, University of Nebraska Softball

"Almost everything in leadership comes back to relationships. The only way you can possibly lead people is to understand people. And the best way to understand them is to get to know them better. I like to have a close relationship with every member of our team."
Mike Krzyzewski, Duke University Men's Basketball Coach

How close should you get with your athletes? Can you ever get too close to your players? Again, each coach is different just as each team is different. You must balance your style and comfort level with what your athletes need. While we do advocate developing close relationships with your athletes, we also insist on making sure that there is a definite line of distinction between yourself and the athlete. After all, as a coach you are a professional who holds a position of power over your athletes. Therefore, it is important that you establish a line of respect with them that you will not cross. Because once you cross this professional line of respect, whether it be by becoming a buddy with your athletes, drinking with them, or developing a romantic relationship, the damage to your credibility, not to mention your team chemistry, is severe and virtually irreparable. We have witnessed or heard of too many situations where coaches blurred or blatantly stepped over the line. In virtually every situation, there were terrible consequences for both the coach and the team. Therefore, while you certainly want to build a close relationship, it is absolutely critical to maintain your professionalism at all times.

We encourage you to get as close as possible to the necessary line between yourself and your athletes, but never to cross it, at least until they are finished playing for you. Then and only then can your relationship be more on an even level.

Also, when you get very close to players, you must guard against favoritism. You will bond with some players more than others. You must be careful not to accord them any special privileges or status. You cannot let your individual relationship with a player cloud your judgment when it comes to the team's overall success.

You Can Call Me "Coach..."

One way that coaches attempt to balance their closeness and their professionalism is how they like their athletes to refer to them. Traditionally, it is customary for athletes to use the title "Coach" when referring to their leaders. This formal title helps to establish a line of respect between the two.

However, some coaches, in an effort to build a closer and more comfortable relationship with their athletes, request that they call the coach by their first name. Coach Summitt says, "I insist on being just "Pat" to our players and staff. It sounds like you can come into my office and talk with me. You might not feel comfortable talking to Coach, or Head Coach, or Mrs. Summitt."

Similarly, we prefer that athletes call us by our first names instead of Mr. Janssen or Dr. Dale. We feel it helps break down the stigma that is sometimes present with our positions and helps us establish a more comfortable and close relationship with the athletes with whom we consult.

In our experience, this first name policy seems to be much more common in women's sports. According to many gender researchers, men usually view the world in a more hierarchical structure and therefore are accustomed to rank and the use of titles. Females on the other hand tend to view relationships in a more interconnected, web-like structure. Perhaps this is the reason why it seems that female coaches are more apt to encourage their players to use their first names.

The key here is that you should do whatever you feel the most comfortable doing. If you feel you are a little more distant with your athletes, you might want to consider encouraging them to use your first name. If you are very close with your athletes, you may want to go by the title of "Coach" to maintain a noticeable line of distinction and respect.

Credible Coaches Develop a Lifetime Loyalty with Their Athletes

"It is cool to see how many former players stop by to see coach. They will come to practice sometime when they are in town. You can tell they respect her and think of her as a friend. I think it will be that way with me too."

College Women's Basketball Player

The third element of caring is what we call loyalty for a lifetime. Not only do credible coaches care about their athletes while they are playing for them, but this affection and interest really extends throughout an athlete's lifetime. As a credible coach, your players will seek your input and counsel when they have major life decisions to make including career, relationships, and family. When the athlete's career is over, the relationship isn't. Many credible coaches actually develop friendships with their former players that last a lifetime. Arizona head track coach Fred Harvey is proud of the lifelong relationships he has developed with his sprinters. He says, "There's not a single athlete who I've coached that I've been close with that I am not in communications with right now."

Think about your former athletes. How many of them call you for advice or make it a point to come by to see you each time they are back in town? If they don't, it might be a good indication that you haven't developed that sense of loyalty that goes beyond sport.

"I had a coach for four years, but I got a friend for life."

Phil Ford on Former Coach Dean Smith

Questions for Reflection

- Do you really care about your athletes?
- How much are you willing to show your athletes that you care?
- What is keeping you from getting closer to your athletes?
- How much do you know about your athletes as people?
- Who is this all about?
- How often do you keep in touch with your former athletes?

Chapter Ten Key Points

- Show your athletes that you genuinely care about them.
- Make your athletes the priority instead of yourself.
- Demonstrate a lifetime of caring and loyalty to your athletes.

ROY WILLIAMS

Head Men's Basketball Coach
University of North Carolina

On Character

When I tell kids something, I want them to be able to depend on it. They know that North Carolina basketball and my family are the two most important things in the world to me. They know that I'll never put my personal goals or wishes in front of what's best for our program. I think that trust there is something that really is important.

Coach Smith told me to be myself. I don't think you can put on any show and fool kids. Because they can see through that so I think it is extremely important just to be yourself.

I think trust has to be there. You get it at different levels with different coaches, but to me it's most important. That loyalty, that feeling that we're in this thing together is the most important thing with our team. So people might not emphasize it as much as I do, and that's not to say that that they're wrong because that might not be comfortable for them. But, for me, when I'm working with somebody I'm going to be fiercely loyal to them, and I want that same kind of loyalty back.

On Competence

For me it's a learning experience all the time. Anytime there's a basketball game on, I don't watch as just a spectator. I'm always paying attention and trying to see if there's something new and different that I could get from them.

On Commitment

Make sure that you are working enough yourself that you're not surprised. If you're prepared, you've watched your tapes, you've done the things that you need to do, and you're not surprised, then that will automatically mean that there's enough respect there with your players.

On Caring

I tell every youngster that when you sign with North Carolina I'm going to be concerned about you for the rest of your life.

I want my players to remember that I cared about them and not just their number of points and rebounds. And that I did know a little about the game. And that the well-being of our team was so much more important than my own individual stuff.

On Consistency

We allow the seniors to make the rules, whether it is curfew or how to dress or whatever, and then we enforce them. I think that the rules that we give them are very simple and ones they can handle.

Gail Goestenkors, Head Women's Basketball Coach, Duke University

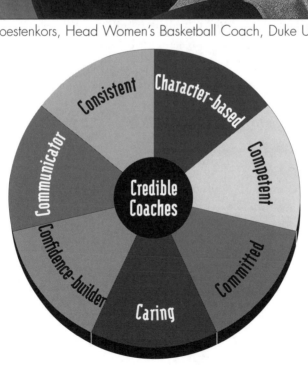

CHAPTER ELEVEN

Credible Coaches Are CONFIDENCE-BUILDERS

How To Get Your Athletes to Perform With Confidence

"You have to create an environment where everybody feels good about themselves and what they can do."

Marty Schottenheimer, San Diego Chargers

Some years ago, a young boy growing up in a small town in northeastern Wisconsin tried out for the eighth grade football team. As a seventh grader the previous year, he spent the season as a seldom-used, third-string quarterback. Realizing that he didn't have much of a future as a quarterback, the boy joined the tight ends and receivers group for the first week of eighth grade practice, hoping to catch a break at a new position.

After a taking a few reps, the boy saw the head coach, Lari DeBruin, walk over to observe the group. As many athletes do when a coach watches them, the boy could feel his heart racing and his palms sweating. He wanted so much to impress Coach DeBruin with a spectacular catch and perhaps earn a starting spot with the first team. The boy ran his route, but because of his nervousness and anxiety, he dropped a perfectly thrown pass.

Hesitantly, the boy looked up at Coach DeBruin fearing his reaction. Coach DeBruin motioned for the boy to come over. With his head down the boy thought, "Oh no, either he is going to cut me from the team or I will spend the year as a third-string bench-warmer again."

Reluctantly, the boy went over to where the coach stood. Coach DeBruin put his arm around the boy and said, "Son, I don't think you have what it takes to be a receiver." The boy believed that his worst fears had been confirmed. He was sure he was going to be cut from the team. Coach DeBruin went on, "Since you don't seem to be the receiver type, I'm going to make you my running back."

The boy was both shocked and amazed as Coach DeBruin led him over to the running backs group. "Running back?" he thought to himself. "If I couldn't make it as a quarterback or a receiver, how am I ever going to make it as a running back?" Despite the boy's doubts, Coach DeBruin saw something in him that he couldn't see at that time.

Coach DeBruin patiently coached the boy in this new position. The boy made a lot of mistakes at first, but eventually learned what he needed to do. Bolstered by Coach DeBruin's belief and confidence in him, the boy slowly began seeing himself as the team's running back. With his coach's encouragement and compliments, the boy's confidence grew exponentially. Somehow in roughly two weeks time, Coach DeBruin transformed a third-string player with little confidence into the team's starting running back. The boy even managed to lead the team in rushing for the season.

Now unfortunately this story does not have a Cinderella-type ending because the boy did not go on to win the Heisman trophy nor did he even play in college. However, while his football career was relatively short-lived, the spark of confidence that Coach DeBruin ignited in the boy back in eighth grade still burns brightly within him to this very day. So much so that the boy eventually chose a career in the sporting world which allowed him to study credible coaches and inspired him to co-author the book you are now reading. (Thanks Coach DeBruin for the positive impact you made on me and the lives of so many young people!)

Confidence is Critical

We share Jeff's personal story with you to remind you about the awesome power your confidence in athletes can have on them. The confidence you show in your athletes often makes or breaks their confidence. This concept is so important we feel we must repeat it. The confidence you show in your athletes often makes or breaks their confidence. Your words and actions have the ability to either build your athletes' confidence or destroy it.

Credible coaches are confidence builders; they see the potential in each of their athletes and help them realize it. Through their words and actions, successful coaches communicate confidence to their players and help them see and fulfill the untapped potential inside of them.

Confidence obviously is one of the most important mental characteristics an athlete needs for success. Arizona softball coach Mike Candrea believes that 90% of the game of softball, and all sports for that matter, is confidence. Therefore, because confidence is so important, Coach Candrea often tells coaches, "Your job is to put smiles on your players' faces."

Athletes who play with confidence can achieve some amazing things. Confident athletes are aggressive and look to make things happen. They trust themselves and their abilities. When adversity strikes, confident athletes maintain their composure and stay mentally tough. Confident athletes want to perform when the game is on the line because they know they have a great chance of coming through in the clutch.

Conversely, athletes who lack confidence become tense in pressure situations and often choke. They play not to lose rather than playing to win. They are constantly looking over their shoulders because they fear making mistakes. When mistakes do occur, athletes who lack confidence get easily frustrated and down on themselves, sometimes for the rest of the competition. You can see then why confidence is such an important mental characteristic to instill in your players.

Confidence is Fragile: Handle With Care

The challenge with building confidence is that it is such a fragile construct for many athletes. "I've realized in the last five years that kids come in here less confident and more fragile," says Coach Pat Summitt. Even former San Francisco 49ers great Joe Montana, one of football's all-time greatest quarterbacks, admitted, "Confidence is a fragile thing." An athlete might be confident one minute and then a play or two later her confidence could be shattered. An athlete's confidence often fluctuates considerably throughout the course of a season and even throughout a practice or competition.

Further, sport involves a great deal of failure. On average, soccer and hockey players miss roughly 90% of the shots they attempt, softball and baseball hitters are out 70% of the time, basketball players miss 50% of their shots, and quarterbacks don't complete 40% of the passes they attempt. Therefore all of this natural failure tends to erode an athlete's confidence. If athletes are not able to cope with the inevitable failure they must face and stay confident, the game will swallow them.

"How a player deals with the failure that is built into the game eventually determines how successful they will be."

Mike Candrea, University of Arizona Softball

Confidence is obviously important for younger athletes when they are just beginning. Young athletes need a lot of patience, encouragement, support, and compliments as they build both their skills and confidence. Youth sport coaches need to spend as much time building confidence as they do sport skills.

However, even college and professional athletes regularly struggle with their confidence and rely on their coaches to help them build it. For example, NBA superstar Grant Hill credits Duke men's basketball coach Mike Krzyzewski with helping him develop the confidence necessary to make it to the NBA. Hill says, "Coach K felt I was better than I ever believed I could be. He constantly reassured me. And he was always patient. With time, he helped me develop my skills as a player and he helped me gain the confidence I needed to make it to the NBA."

As Grant Hill admits, even elite athletes doubt themselves and struggle with their confidence from time to time. Injuries, poor training, performance slumps, moving up to a higher level, hostile crowds, hypercritical sportswriters, and big games, are just some of the reasons why athletes doubt themselves. Virtually all high school and college freshmen athletes experience a period of time when they wonder if they really have what it takes to compete at the next level. All athletes are continually faced with challenges that cause them to question their confidence. Therefore, the key is not eliminating all doubts and fear, but mustering up enough confidence and courage to perform despite the doubts and distractions.

Your Confidence Becomes Their Confidence

Ideally athletes should be able to create confidence on their own by focusing on their personal strengths, past successes, and hard work. In reality many athletes rely heavily on their coaches for their confidence. Your athletes often depend on your compliments and encouragement to help them feel confident because many have a difficult time encouraging and complimenting themselves.

In talking with athletes, we have found that a significant number of them base their confidence largely on how much they perceive their coach is confident in them. Of course the key word is perceive. Your athletes will base their confidence on how much confidence they perceive you have in them as opposed to your actual level of confidence in them. We know of several instances where athletes thought that their coaches had lost confidence in them when in actuality this was not the case. Many times the athletes misinterpreted the coach's comments, tone, body language, or silence to mean that the coach had lost confidence in them. Therefore, you must be conscious that almost everything you do, say, or don't say, can have an impact on your athletes' confidence.

Although a coach's confidence in an athlete is important for both genders, in our experience, female athletes rely on their coaches even more so for confidence. We believe this occurs because society teaches males to project confidence from an early age and not to rely on others as much. However, society teaches females to base their confidence on others' external evaluations of them. Therefore, if you are coaching female athletes, you need to be especially attuned to your athletes' confidence.

A Word to the Wise:
Building Confidence is Like Spinning Plates

Because you play such a prominent role in both the development and maintenance of your athletes' confidence, it is up to you to continually monitor each of your player's confidence on a consistent basis. You want to proactively build confidence so that it becomes as solid and stable as possible. Also, you must be able to repair and rebuild an athlete's confidence when she begins to struggle.

Florida volleyball coach Mary Wise uses an analogy of a circus performer spinning plates on sticks as a way to talk about the coach's role of monitoring and building each athlete's confidence. The performer starts by getting the first plate spinning and then proceeds down the line to spin the rest of the plates. Once all of the plates are spinning, the performer then needs to monitor each plate to make sure that it is spinning effectively. When the performer spots a plate that is beginning to slow down or wobble, she focuses her attention on it and gives it another spin to keep it from crashing to the floor. Similarly, coaches must monitor and spin their athletes' plates to keep them feeling confident and good about themselves. If the coach spots someone whose confidence plate is slowing down or beginning to wobble, it is part of the coach's job to spin the person's plate providing some encouragement and support. Coach Wise and her staff talk about spinning an athlete's plate when they see someone who is struggling and in need of a confidence booster. She says, "Coaching is all about spinning plates. If I ignore an athlete for too long, she'll crash. And when they crash it's so hard to pick up the pieces."

SEVEN STEPS TO BUILDING YOUR ATHLETES' CONFIDENCE

1. Focus on Potential
2. Plant Seeds of Success
3. Sell Athletes on Themselves
4. Show Them a Simple and Specific Plan
5. Inspire Them to Work Hard
6. Set Them Up for Early Success
7. Accentuate the Positive

1. Focus on Potential: What You See is What You Eventually Get

How do you build your athletes' confidence? To begin with, you must first focus on your athletes' potential. Building confidence begins with seeing the potential in your athletes, even though they may not always see it in themselves. It is said that the great Italian sculptor Michelangelo could see the beautiful statue of David already completed in his mind when all he had before him was a block of stone. Similarly, successful coaches envision polished athletes even though all they have in front of them are players who are quite raw.

Unfortunately, seeing an athlete's potential can be a tough task for many coaches. It is far too easy to be blinded by athletes' glaring short-comings and liabilities than it is to see their future potential. Too many coaches get caught up on what their athletes presently can't do and let it dominate their thinking. As former UCLA basketball coach John Wooden once said, "Don't let what you cannot do interfere with what you can do." Obviously this saying also applies to coaches—Don't let what your athletes cannot do interfere with what they can do.

Favorite Athlete Exercise

There's a simple exercise we like to do in our Credible Coaching workshops to illustrate a point about your athletes' potential. All you need to do is think of one of your favorite athletes. Using the following list of characteristics, circle all of the ones that you feel he or she possesses:

hard worker, positive attitude, team player, mentally tough, leader

Now think of one of your least favorite athletes. Again using the same following list, circle all of the characteristics that you feel he or she possesses:

hard worker, positive attitude, team player, mentally tough, leader

If you are like most coaches, you have several qualities circled for your favorite athlete and few if any characteristics circled for your least favorite athlete. However, and this is the point of the exercise, each of the athletes possesses and is capable of demonstrating many if not all of the positive characteristics. Your favorite athletes presently show these important characteristics. Your least favorite athletes are not displaying these characteristics at this time. Your challenge is to bring these positive characteristics out of your least favorite athletes.

---

2. Plant Seeds of Success

Once you get a positive picture of what an athlete could become, you then must help him see the same picture. Credible coaches invest their time planting seeds of success in their athletes' minds. Coach DeBruin planted a seed of success in Jeff's mind when he said, "You're going to be my running back." Arizona head track coach Fred Harvey planted a seed of success in 400 meter sprinter Carolyn Jackson's mind by telling her that she was a "53 seconder" even though at the time her previous best was 58 seconds. Arizona Softball coach Mike Candrea plants seeds of success in his players' minds when he tells them, "This team is special."

"If you talk to most of my athletes, I have more belief in what they are capable of doing than they do. They need to see that confidence with me and I need to show them why I believe in them."

Fred Harvey, Head Track Coach, University of Arizona

"For most people, it's not what they are that holds them back. It's what they think they're not."

John Maxwell, Author of *Becoming a Person of Influence*

"Our chief want is someone who will inspire us to be what we know we could be."

Ralph Waldo Emerson

While Florida basketball coach Billy Donovan is one of the nation's rising stars, he didn't begin that way. In 1985 Donovan had just finished his sophomore season at Providence College and planned to transfer when Rick Pitino took over the program. However, Pitino told him he had a shot at being a good player if he would only take responsibility for his own success, drop 30 pounds over the summer, and get in the best shape of his life. Donovan did as Pitino instructed. When Donovan showed up in the fall of his junior year, Pitino dressed him up in a cowboy outfit and put him on the cover of their game programs as "Billy the Kid." With this new-found confidence and persona, Donovan went from a pudgy player who lacked the size and speed to compete in the Big East to an all-conference player who led Providence to the Final Four. The confidence that Coach Pitino helped instill in Donovan back then continues to show itself today in his coaching career.

Similarly, former Northwestern and Colorado football coach Gary Barnett believes that the essence of coaching is to take people to a higher level. He created a mission statement with his coaches at Northwestern which read: "Our mission is to take the student-athlete where he cannot take himself." Barnett knows all about the importance of planting seeds of success. He took over the dismal Northwestern football program in the early 1990's and proclaimed he would help take the "Purple to Pasadena" for the Rose Bowl. Despite Northwestern being one of the worst teams at the time, Barnett continually emphasized his successful vision for the team. He put up signs all around the offices, locker room, and weight room saying "Belief Without Evidence." His main message was that his players needed to believe in the team even though they really had every reason not to based on their past history of losing. He had his players sing the song "High Hopes" and chant "Rose Bowl" when they finished their practices to remind the team of their ultimate goal. In a remarkable four seasons, Barnett engineered one of the biggest turnarounds in college football history as he led Northwestern from a perennial last place finish in the Big Ten to the conference championship and the Rose Bowl.

Planting seeds of success is a clear way of showing your athletes that you believe in them. They might think you are crazy at first, but the confidence you show in them is usually the catalyst that gets them believing in themselves.

"Coach Summitt told me she'd never seen a player at my position do the things I could do, and she said that I could be the best player ever to play for her at Tennessee. At first I was thinking, 'Dag! This lady is nuts!' But inside I knew that if you have somebody who believes in you, you can do almost anything, and Coach Summitt really seemed to believe in me."

Chamique Holdsclaw, Los Angeles Sparks

"When people realize that someone has faith in them... productivity usually increases. We have a natural desire to not want to disappoint those who believe in us and trust us."

Tom Osborne, Former University of Nebraska Football Coach

3. Sell Athletes on Themselves: Help them Feel Capable

"Coach could sell anything to anyone. He has a way of making you feel like you can do anything you want."

College Men's Basketball Player

It's one thing to have high expectations for your athletes, it's another thing to get them to believe that they are capable of achieving those expectations. Credible coaches build confidence by selling athletes on their own unique abilities and talents. They help athletes reach beyond their own self-imposed doubts, limits, and fears to pursue their dreams. There is an old saying, "I love you not because of who you are, but how you make me feel about myself." Credible coaches take this saying to heart and seek to make their athletes feel competent, capable, important, appreciated, and special. Florida volleyball coach Mary Wise says, "I work real hard at developing my players' confidence and making them feel good about themselves. When they feel pretty good about themselves I think there is a lot they can accomplish."

Denver Broncos running back Terrell Davis believes that coach Mike Shanahan's confidence in his players has a big impact on their success. "He makes us all feel like first-round picks who are capable of anything. Mike has a way of making people feel important. He makes it as comfortable for his players as possible, so that when you're out there playing, you're playing for him."

4. Give Them a Specific and Simple Plan to Succeed

Once they are inspired, show your athletes what they will need to do to reach their goals and potential. Show them the steps they will need to take on a daily, weekly, and monthly basis. Develop a specific yet simple plan that will take them from where they are now to where they can and should be down the road. You want to break down your vision of what they could be into a realistic plan that they can follow today.

This same process works when you are trying to build your team's confidence during tournament time or when you are facing a team that seems tough to beat. Give your team a specific, workable plan to follow and you will be amazed at the results. Jody Adams, a guard on Tennessee's 1991 national championship team and current assistant coach at the University of Missouri-Kansas City, remembers how Coach Summitt instilled confidence in the Lady Vols. "Pat was very organized and she always had a plan for us. We went into the NCAA tournament thinking we were supposed to win it. We believed in Pat and her plan so much that we could have been matched up against Michael Jordan and the Chicago Bulls and still thought we were going to win the championship."

5. Emphasize Working Hard and Deserving Success

One of the best phrases from Rick Pitino's book *Success is a Choice* is that coaches and athletes need to "Deserve Victory." Pitino insists that the only way people can achieve true success is by good old-fashioned hard work. When you feel like you have outworked your opponents, you feel you deserve to be successful because you earned it more than they have.

You have to convince your athletes that hard work is something that is good for them. All the sweat, aches, pains, and exhaustion is not a sacrifice—instead it is an investment in their potential. They have to feel that each time they go the extra mile that they are gaining an advantage on their competition. Credible coaches make their athletes feel that no one is a harder worker, more prepared, or more ready than they are.

6. Set People Up for Early Success

The best way to help athletes to feel good about themselves is to intentionally set them up for early success. Credible coaches structure practices and arrange their schedules to build in small early successes. They understand that confidence is most fragile when their athletes are first learning. They want their athletes to experience the sweet taste of success early so that they yearn for more of it.

Of course, this doesn't necessarily mean that you have to schedule several "cream puff" opponents. However, you should not load up on a bunch of heavy weights early in your season if your team's confidence is fragile. Too many early losses could destroy your athletes' confidence for the rest of the season.

"Work on success first and let them succeed. Good coaches put their players in a position where they can succeed. Don't put your players in a position where they're just going to fail miserably."

Mary Wise, University of Florida Volleyball

"Coaching athletes is about what you want them to achieve and never allowing their confidence to be stomped into the ground. Because once you stomp it down there it is so hard to get back."

Fred Harvey, Head Track Coach, University of Arizona

7. Accentuate the Positive

"Coach does a great job of pointing out the positives. Don't get me wrong, she can get on you when you screw up, but it's more positive than it is negative."

College Women's Lacrosse Player

When athletes are successful, credible coaches look to catch people doing things right and praise them publicly for it. They help people believe in themselves by accentuating their strengths. This allows people to develop a solid foundation of confidence from which they can build in the future.

In contrast, coercive coaches focus on people's failures and weaknesses. When they occur, coercive coaches are quick to point out mistakes and harp on them in an effort to scare or embarrass athletes into not repeating them. They set people up to fail and when it occurs they say, "See, I told you that you couldn't do this."

"Great leaders inflate the people around them. Poor leaders deflate the people around them."

Rick Pitino, University of Louisville Men's Basketball Coach

Using Pitino's analogy, consider whether you spend more of your time inflating or deflating your athletes. How often do you use the following phrases?

You can do this.
I believe in you.
Trust yourself.

I love the way you...

You are a great athlete because...

I wish every coach could have a chance to coach an athlete like you.

HOW TO CORRECT AND CRITICIZE YOUR ATHLETES WITHOUT DESTROYING THEIR CONFIDENCE

"Coach can get on us when we need it! But, he really tries to be positive with us for the most part. He lets us know when we do something wrong, but he also lets us know when we do things well. One thing I really respect about coach is the way he teaches and talks to us. He treats us with respect and really is a good teacher."

High School Baseball Player

Obviously it is much easier to build your athletes' confidence when they are performing well. Unfortunately sports and life aren't always going to be easy and successful. It is unrealistic and impossible to expect you to be positive and complimentary of your athletes 24 hours a day, seven days a week. There are going to be times when you need to correct them after they make mistakes. There will be many times when you are upset with them because of a lack of effort or their failure to abide by the team rules. Duke men's basketball coach Mike Krzyzewski probably says it best when he says, "This isn't all about 'I love you,' and 'Let's hold hands and skip.' It's also about 'Get your rear in gear,' 'What the hell are you doing?' and 'Why aren't you in class?'"

Many athletes admit that their coaches need to be hard on them at times to get their attention. One athlete said, "It can't all be peaches and cream. Coach has to yell at us sometimes because that is what some guys respond to in certain situations."

Therefore the big questions become—How do you correct your athletes without them getting down on themselves? How do you communicate with them when you are upset with them? How do you maintain your athletes' confidence when they are struggling? And finally, how can you constructively criticize them without breaking their spirit? The real trick of coaching is knowing how to preserve your athletes' confidence when you need to criticize and correct them.

Different Strokes for Different Folks

Unfortunately there is not one set way to coach every person. Coaches must remember that each person is unique. The true art of coaching depends on discovering how each of your players is motivated. Since no two athletes are exactly alike, so too must you coach each person a little differently. Although baseball manager Gene Mauch once said that it's easier for 25 players to understand one manager than one manger to understand 25 players, managers like Joe Torre of the Yankees and Skip Bertman of LSU have been very successful by taking the exact opposite approach. It would be much easier to force all of your athletes to totally adapt to you, however, credible coaches invest the time to get to know each of their players on a personal level, so that they can find out what makes them tick, and adapt their coaching to suit their athletes' needs.

"As a manager, a high level of sensitivity will help you make snap decisions about what to say, how to say it, and when to say it. Some of your players require unconditional support. Others need to be massaged. Still others need to be pushed to work harder. Everyone needs attention."

Joe Torre, New York Yankees

"You must understand the uniqueness of each individual. There are different push-buttons on every athlete. That's what we try really hard to do is find what are those buttons with each individual player. It's extremely important to know when can you push them and when you have to back off."

Mary Wise, University of Florida Volleyball

How do you discover the best way to coach and motivate each person? First, you need to find out their goals. Do they play because they love to compete, desire to please other people, want to win championships, or seek to earn a college scholarship or professional contract? To help you better understand what motivates your athletes, we encourage you to sit down with each of them and ask them. You'll find that each athlete has different motivations for playing. Once you understand their goals, you will understand how to motivate them appropriately.

When you are asking your athletes about their goals, we also suggest that you ask them about how they like to be coached in various situations. For example, you might ask them, "How can I best help you reach your goals?" "What can I say or do that will help motivate you?" "What can I do when you are struggling to help get you back on track?" The answers to these questions should give you great insights on how you can best coach each of your athletes.

Secondly, in order to motivate your athletes you need to understand how much confidence they have in themselves. The confidence level of each athlete largely dictates how you need to coach him or her. If athletes have a solid and stable base of confidence you can challenge them a lot more. Confident people have a strong sense of themselves so you can push them much more than athletes with low confidence. Conversely, athletes with low confidence are much more sensitive. If you challenge them too much they tend to get down on themselves and discouraged. They take criticism personally.

"You can push people with high self-esteem harder. Because they feel good about themselves, you can set very high expectations for them and invariably they will meet those expectations. There's nothing they feel they can't accomplish. Conversely people with low self-esteem tend to be fragile. They tend to doubt themselves, thus when criticized they have a tendency to deflate, as if the very criticism simply reinforces their own image of themselves."

Rick Pitino, University of Louisville Men's Basketball

Coaching the Fragile Athlete: Be Supportive and Patient

As you get to know your individual athletes, you will find that some of them are highly sensitive people. These are the athletes who immediately look at you for your reaction when they make mistakes. They tend to crumble when they are criticized because they have little to no self-confidence to fall back on. Take a moment to think about who these athletes might be on your team.

Based on our experiences, we would estimate that anywhere from 25 to 33% or more of the athletes on your team might be categorized as fragile athletes. With these more sensitive athletes, you must be very careful about what you say to them, the tone of voice you use, and your body language. As we mentioned earlier, because these athletes lack confidence, they tend to look directly to you to provide it for them. If you don't want them to get down on themselves, you must stay positive when they make mistakes. Their confidence is already tenuous so the last thing you want to do is yell at them. Instead, help them focus on the mental or physical adjustment they need to make to perform successfully on their next attempt. Athletes with fragile confidence need a great deal of your understanding, patience, and support.

Many coaches have a low tolerance for athletes with low self-confidence and regard them as "high maintenance" athletes. They have to be careful with them and spend a lot of time developing their confidence. Therefore it is very easy to get frustrated with these athletes, move them to the second team, or cut them altogether. However, you risk losing a potential gold mine if you are too hasty in your decisions about these types of athletes.

"One of your tasks as a manager is to send positive messages to a team player who undercuts himself with negative thinking."

Joe Torre, New York Yankees

Coaching The Confident Athlete: Demand Excellence

Once you help your athletes build a solid base of confidence, only then can you take them to a higher level by demanding more from them. Goethe once said, "Treat a person as they are and they will stay that way. However, treat a person like what they could be and they will become it."

Athletes often describe credible coaches as being very demanding people. They continually push their athletes, urging and encouraging them to attain higher levels of performance. Mediocrity is something that credible coaches absolutely hate; they won't settle for anything less than the athlete's best. Tennessee women's basketball coach Pat Summitt says, "I ask our players to give more of themselves than they think is possible. I know they have more inside of them. I know it. That's why I set such high standards for them."

Credible coaches demand excellence from their athletes. They understand that winning is a habit. Therefore they cultivate that habit by insisting that players give their best at all times—whether it is a practice situation, lifting in the weight room, or playing for the national championship. Slacking off is not tolerated.

This focus on excellence extends to the classroom and representing the team in the community as well. The majority of the credible coaches we interviewed have very strict class attendance policies. These come complete with serious consequences if an athlete does not obey. Not only does Coach Summitt insist that her players go to class, but she also requires that her players sit in the first three rows. To paraphrase Vince Lombardi, credible coaches expect their athlete's best effort because they know that excellence is not a sometimes thing, it's an all the time thing.

Knowing When to Push and When to Ease Up

Because they have taken the time to get to know their athletes so well, credible coaches know when to be demanding of their athletes and when to ease up and support them. They know when they should push athletes past their own perceived limitations, fears, and laziness to help them achieve breakthroughs to higher levels of performance. They also know when to ease up, provide more support, and build people up again. They can sense when a person might be getting too frustrated or discouraged and take the time to encourage them. As a coach, you want to push your athletes hard, but you definitely don't want to break their spirit.

"Pat would push you very hard but she also knew when she needed to reel you back in and give you some more confidence," said Jody Adams about her former coach Pat Summitt. In our interview with Coach Summitt she explained, "I always tell myself, 'Don't ever break their spirit.' I challenge them hard on the practice court to see what they're made out of. And then I recognize I have to go back before we are ready to compete and say, 'Look, I know I've been on you; I know I've challenged you. But I did it for a reason. We have to have you mentally tough and focused for this game."

Credible coaches discover each of their athletes' breaking points. They knowingly push their athletes up to the edge of it and then know when to back off and help them feel more confident.

"It's important to strike the right balance between commending and criticizing... Too much praise loses its effectiveness—just as too much criticism does... The best way to maintain the credibility of compliments and criticism is to use them meaningfully. Don't overuse them."

Pat Summitt, University of Tennessee Women's Basketball

"The more she learned about me, the more Coach Summitt knew how to push my buttons, and she pushed them, again and again and again, in my four years at Tennessee. Sometimes she made me furious. Sometimes she made me cry. Almost all the time, though, she made me play my best."

Chamique Holdsclaw, Washington Mystics

12 TIPS FOR CHALLENGING ATHLETES AND MAINTAINING CONFIDENCE

Here are 12 tips that will help you preserve your athletes' confidence when you need to give them feedback following their mistakes.

1. Be Understanding

First, remember that the vast majority of mistakes athletes make are not intentional (even though at times it might seem otherwise). Athletes want to play well not only for themselves, but many of them want to please their coaches and teammates too. The mistakes they make are not because they want to make them, but more often because they have not sufficiently mastered the skill, do not understand the strategy, or are overwhelmed by the pressure of the moment.

Most athletes are already upset when they make a mistake and become overly tough on themselves. Some take this to the extreme. This is especially true of your perfectionist athletes who are overly critical of themselves following mistakes. If you too come down on them hard for their mistakes you only compound the problem rather than help them solve it.

"I think what every manager or coach needs is an understanding heart; because when a player doesn't do well, the manager or coach has got to understand how that player feels. That player probably feels worse than anybody, and that manager or coach has to understand that."

Tommy Lasorda, Former Los Angeles Dodgers Manager

Therefore when your athletes make a mistake, initially you should support them and encourage them to correct it. If you look to criticize or demean your athletes immediately, they will likely lose confidence, play tentatively because they fear making another mistake, and become defensive and resent your criticism.

2. Allow Athletes to Play Through Mistakes Whenever Possible

One of the best things you can do to demonstrate your confidence in your athletes is allow them to play through their mistakes whenever possible. Give them the chance to correct themselves within the game rather than always pulling them out or offering your feedback right away. Allowing athletes to self correct and learn from mistakes helps them learn how to be resilient.

In a somewhat extreme example, former Nebraska volleyball coach Terry Pettit never pulled his setter from a match. He says, "In 23 years I never subbed a setter. Never once took her out of a game. That's trust. I never had a situation where a setter was looking over wondering, 'Does he trust me?' She never had to worry about, 'How does he feel about me today?' or if my future depended upon this set." Pettit trusted his setter enough that he would not pull her regardless of the situation. Granted, Pettit was able to recruit some pretty effective setters, but to never replace them increased the athletes' trust in themselves (and Pettit) on the court.

If you pull your athletes or chastise them every time they make a mistake, they will learn to play tentatively. The quickest way to create a fear of failure in athletes is to punish them when they fail. Pulling an athlete immediately after a mistake will be viewed as punishment by many of your athletes. They will be more worried about making mistakes and getting pulled than they are focused on making plays.

"Make sure that your players get the opportunity to work through mistakes, to get that second or third or fourth opportunity if they're having a tough game. By the end of the day, they're likely to have success because you believe in them."

Tom Renney, Director of Player Personnel, New York Rangers

3. Avoid Making It Personal—Criticize the Behavior, Not the Person

When giving criticism, make sure the target of it is the athlete's behavior and not the actual athlete himself. For example, let's say an athlete makes a mistake at a critical time. You want to criticize the behavior—"Mike that wasn't a very smart pass to make in that situation because..." versus "Mike you are such an idiot. How could you be so stupid?"

Criticizing the behavior allows a person to keep his confidence intact because behavior can be changed and corrected. However, if you criticize him as a person, he can't help but take it personally.

4. Limit Your Use of Profanity

Why do some coaches feel that they have to curse at athletes to get them to perform? We have asked many coaches about this and their typical responses are: "It helps me make a point." "The athlete knows I am serious when I curse." "It is the kind of language some of these kids grew up around and it's what they respond to best." "A good #$%*&% every now and then really gets their attention." "We are preparing them for battle. It is a war out there and they need to be tough."

We would agree that you can get the attention of your athletes with a periodic curse word. But, we would also argue that cursing at athletes does very little for your credibility with them. They will not respect you if you curse at them personally. There are many ways you can get your point across to someone without using profanity.

Ralph Sabock, author of *Coaching: A Realistic Perspective* offers a "tongue in cheek" list of reasons coaches swear. He attempts to demonstrate how swearing can affect your athletes and your image as an educated person. Following are a few of those reasons.

a. It is an example of self-control.

b. It demonstrates my command of the English language.

c. It shows how tough I am.

d. It makes me a better teacher.

e. It makes people respect me.

f. It adds dignity to my role as a coach.

g. It demonstrates how much I respect you.

In our workshops with coaches we ask them if they consider themselves teachers as well as coaches. An overwhelming majority indicate they view themselves as teachers first. They indicate that they take pride in teaching athletes how to execute skills. The reality is that if you are a coach, you are a teacher as well. Teachers in the classroom would not be able to curse at their students and retain their jobs for very long. Granted, sport is a more intense environment than teaching in the classroom, but if you work on it, you can get your message across just as effectively without lacing it with curse words.

5. Never embarrass an athlete in public.

You have probably heard the phrase "Praise in public, criticize in private." It is a saying that you as a leader need to live by. When you praise athletes in front of their peers or in the media, it does a lot to build their confidence. However, when you criticize athletes in public, you embarrass them in front of their peers.

Darrell Royal, the legendary former football coach at the University of Texas, says that a mistake coaches often make very early in their careers is to berate or criticize an athlete in front of his teammates. He feels that if you do this on a regular basis you will destroy that athlete's pride. Which if you think about it, is the one thing you will be relying on when the going gets tough. No one likes to be singled out and berated in front of others. Somehow this concept gets lost on some coaches when they communicate with athletes. They forget that they would not want to be treated in that manner.

"I never embarrass or humiliate a team player in front of others."

Joe Torre, New York Yankees

6. Avoid using sarcasm to embarrass athletes into performing better.

Saying things like, "What's wrong with mommy's little boy today?" "Come on stone hands, can't you catch anything?" and "You are the worst example of an athlete I have ever seen" don't really motivate people to perform better. Making comments like this only undermines your credibility as an effective coach. Coaches who do this give the impression they do not know how to handle their frustrations with an athlete. When you use sarcasm, your athletes will disdain you and will not enjoy playing for you.

7. Use the "sandwich approach" when providing feedback.

What happens if an administrator, a colleague, or a loved one always seems to find fault in what you are doing before they mention anything good that you are doing? You probably become defensive right away and begin to tune them out. Your athletes will respond the same way to you if you always begin your feedback with something they are doing wrong. Using the sandwich approach requires you to begin your interaction with something positive. You then instruct the athlete on what needs to be corrected or changed. And, you end the interaction with a positive statement. For example, "James, I really appreciate your effort. If you will extend more with your hands, you will get more of those rebounds. Come on now I know you can do this."

8. "I Know You're Better Than That"

One of the best things you can say to your athletes when they are making mistakes and not performing well is, "I know you're better than that." This simple phrase tells them that you know they are capable of performing much better than what they are currently showing. It clearly communicates to them that they are not performing up to your expectations, but more importantly, you believe they have the ability to be playing at a higher level. A key here is to be aware of how you say it. If it is said in a sarcastic tone, it will lose its effectiveness. You have to be enthusiastic and say it in a way that will be perceived as positive by your athletes.

9. Focus on the Solution

Instead of focusing on the problem, help athletes focus on the solution. When athletes are struggling, help them focus on the physical and or mental adjustments they need to make to be successful. One of Arizona softball coach Mike Candrea's patented sayings to his players is "Make an adjustment." By saying this, Candrea wants to take his players' focus away from the mistake and on to the correction they plan to make.

10. Make it a "We" Project

Florida volleyball coach Mary Wise believes that there is support in numbers. For example, when one of her athletes is struggling, Coach Wise and the athlete tackle the problem together. Instead of saying "You need to do this," or "You need to do that," Coach Wise makes it a "we" project.

For example, if one of your athletes needs to develop more strength you can tell him, "We need to get you stronger." Or if another of your athletes is having trouble in the classroom you can say "We need to get your grades up." Making it a "we" project shows your athletes that you are willing to partner with them to help them improve.

11. Remind them of their Strengths, Past Successes, and Preparation

In addition to your praise, athletes can build their own confidence by focusing on three major areas: their strengths, past successes they have achieved, and their preparation. However, most athletes forget about these things when they struggle and instead focus on the opposite: their weaknesses, past failures, and poor preparation. Thus, one of the best things you can do is to remind them of what they already have going for them. Refocus your athletes on their strengths. Remind them of past games or practices where they were successful because if they have done it once before, they can do it again. A great way to do this is to put together a highlight video for your athletes of their past successful performances. Finally, remind them of all the work that they have put in and that they deserve to be successful because they have paid the price of success.

12. Don't Give Up—Don't Ever Give Up!

In the immortal words of former North Carolina State men's basketball coach Jimmy Valvano, "Don't give up, don't ever give up!" You must adopt this mindset when it comes to your athletes. The last thing you would ever want to do is to give up on them. If they ever sense you have given up on them, they will either give up on themselves or lose all respect for you and give up on you as a coach.

"I've worked for organizations in the past that are real quick to jump off the bandwagon when things aren't going well... With Joe, you don't really have to look over your shoulder, because you'll lose confidence in yourself long before Joe loses confidence in you."

Mike Stanton, New York Yankees Pitcher on Manager Joe Torre

Show Appreciation

"Coach takes the time to recognize everyone for doing their part. He talks about practice players and the good job they do. He even has had a little ceremony where he has recognized the maintenance guys for their hard work. You could tell it meant a lot to those guys."

College Baseball Player

Finally, as confidence builders, credible coaches appreciate everyone's contribution to the team. They look to make everyone feel that they are special and an important part of the team's success. Typically the coaches are the ones who receive a lot of the credit when teams do well—and much of the blame when they don't. However credible coaches deflect and distribute any credit they might receive back on their athletes, coaching staff, and support staff. Credible coaches want their athletes to be the ones responsible for the team's success. By encouraging the athletes to own the team's success, credible coaches instill the confidence to create future successes.

In addition to sharing the credit for success with their athletes, credible coaches also highly appreciate everyone who is associated with their programs. They make their secretaries, trainers, sports information directors, and custodians feel special because they are an important part of the team. Credible coaches often include these people in team events, pictures, meetings, and memos whenever possible. This of course has a tremendous effect on their confidence, motivation, and allegiance to the team as well.

Conversely, credible coaches look to take much of the blame and criticism when their team is not doing well. Dean Smith often said, "Players win games, coaches lose them." This philosophy also helps your athletes preserve their confidence during tough times because the coach willingly puts himself out to take the heat.

"As long as you give the praise and the support to the athletes who are making a difference, and you are genuine about it, I think the people who follow you will always die for you... Treating your people with this kind of respect, and letting people know why your teams are successful is important... I think that ends up winning the respect of everyone."

Anson Dorrance, University of North Carolina Women's Soccer

"If anything goes bad, I did it.
If anything goes semi-good, then we did it.
If anything goes real good, then you did it.
That's all it takes to get people to win football games."

Bear Bryant, Former Alabama Football Coach

Questions for Reflection

- Whose confidence is fragile on your team? How do you tend to coach them?
- How much confidence do you have in each of your athletes?
- Do you spend more time inflating your athletes or deflating your athletes?
- Have you planted a seed of success in any of your athletes lately?
- How do you help your athletes feel about themselves?
- Do you look to set your athletes up for success?
- Do you know when to push your athletes and when to ease up?
- Can you challenge and correct your athletes without destroying their confidence?
- Do you tell your athletes how much you appreciate them?

Chapter Eleven Key Points

- Inspire your athletes to reach their potential.
- Help your athletes feel good about themselves.
- Demand excellence from your athletes.
- Challenge and support your athletes when they fail.
- Let your athletes know how much you appreciate them.

GAIL GOESTENKORS

Head Women's Basketball Coach
Duke University

On Character

I think that once you've established that credibility with them—you've come down on their level and you're empathetic with them and you communicate with them, and you're honest, and they know what to expect from you—so when you ask them to do this, they're going to be more willing to give everything they have.

On Competence

I think you obviously need to be willing to admit that you don't know everything—and be willing to learn. We are watching tapes constantly—whether it's teaching tapes or game tapes of other teams that we feel they did a good job with a certain aspect of the game. So that you learn to coach and do that you are also able to teach your players new things. Because if you're teaching them the same things over and over they're gonna become bored and you're going to become bored… striving to learn more. Pushing yourself and pushing your team to the limits—finding out how to maximize your potential… you have to push yourself to find out more about yourself

On Caring

I tell my team I love them all the time. I mean I'll be yelling at them, "I love you guys but you are driving me crazy!" But I tell them I love them all the time. I've come a long way because I'm a head coach and learning that it was okay. I started feeling like I'm going to be hugging more and telling them how I care about them and letting them know. Because I don't want these days to pass by and all of a sudden they didn't ever get a hug from me or they didn't feel that I cared about them or knew that I loved them. Definitely I feel that it is a strength of mine now. It certainly was not when I first started.

Help your players understand that you're just there to help them. That's all my job is—to give them the best opportunity to be successful. That's it. And hopefully help them feel they are cared for, they are loved and they are becoming a better player and a better person a better student along the way.

On Confidence Building

I think it comes back to helping them play within their comfort zone. If they're not confident then they're not comfortable. So it's being able to know your players, being able to motivate them, what makes them tick, what's going to push them to excel and not push them over the limit. Being able to yell at them. Whenever we say something to a player, especially when they come out of the game—and I told my assistants they have to say first something positive then make the correction then end with something positive—because they are going to remember the first and last thing you say. But you still have to tell them. I think it is finding that balance because it will be a little bit different with each kid.

On Communication

I think probably as far as dealing with the players, I think communication is probably the number one. We have a lot of individual needs on a basketball team. But, I think communication is the key because we need to find out who they are and what's important to be able to motivate them properly. We all know everybody is motivated in different ways and so I think the biggest thing is to be able to communicate with your staff, with your team to find out who they are.

Dr. Leroy Walker, Former President of the U.S. Olympic Committee

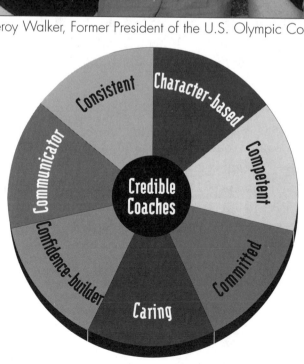

CHAPTER TWELVE

Credible Coaches Are COMMUNICATORS

How To Connect With Your Athletes

"So much of good leadership rests on your ability to get your message across. The ability to communicate effectively is one of your best weapons."

Rick Pitino, University of Louisville Men's Basketball

One of the great things about being a coach is that you have the opportunity to interact with people on a daily basis. Depending on how you handle them, these interactions can go a long way in determining the success of your program. Unfortunately as humans, we aren't always effective communicators. We often make comments we don't mean or later regret. There are times when we expect people to know what we are thinking without having to tell them. We tend to talk more than we listen. And, it is very difficult to receive feedback about something we are doing without becoming defensive. For various reasons, effective communication is a skill that some coaches have not mastered. Many of the problems coaches have with athletes can be attributed to a lack of effective communication between the two. Or as George Bernard Shaw once said, "The greatest problem in communication is the illusion that it has been accomplished."

Fortunately for all of us, effective communication is a skill we can develop. The first step in developing this skill is to view it as important. We have found that credible coaches do take the communication process seriously and strive to effectively communicate with those around them. Credible coaches tend to be open and direct in their communication. They are proactive and seek to resolve potential problems with athletes before they fester into explosive situations. Finally credible coaches invest the time to listen to their athletes and look to involve them in decisions that affect the team.

This is by no means an exhaustive list of the important aspects of effective communication for credible coaching. The topics discussed here are ones that have been mentioned most frequently by the credible coaches and their athletes with whom we have had the privilege of working. After reading this discussion on communication, we hope you will take a critical look at the way you communicate with your athletes and examine your credibility in this important area of coaching.

Open and Direct Communication

"The thing I love about coach is that I really feel like he is up front with us on everything. He always lets us know where we stand and he makes us feel like we can talk to him about almost everything."

College Football Player Talking About His Position Coach

The foundation of effective communication is your ability to be open and direct with your athletes. The messages you send as coach have to be clear and athletes should not have to guess if there are any hidden meanings. You should be very explicit regarding roles athletes play as well as the expectations and standards that you feel are important to the team's success. You can't assume that they know what you are thinking at any time—especially in areas that are vital to success.

As we mentioned in the chapter on character, athletes want their coach to be honest with them regarding their roles. The credible coaches we have come in contact with usually have individual meetings with their athletes as early as possible to explain where each player fits into the bigger picture. By doing this, you can avoid having your athletes feel like you are playing mind games or manipulating them in some way. The same goes for the way you manage your team on a daily basis. Your philosophy and the standards you have for the team must be made clear from the very beginning. Many coaches schedule an initial meeting with their teams to discuss these issues. It is a good idea to provide your philosophy and the standards you expect in writing. Those coaches who must deal with parents also should provide them with your written philosophy statement very early in the season. By having a meeting with parents before the season begins, you will be able to eliminate some of the potential problems they can create for you.

"Confusion leads to misunderstanding, and misunderstanding leads to conflict. You can prevent a load of trouble by making sure your meanings and actions are clearly understood."

Joe Torre, New York Yankees

In addition to being open and direct with your athletes, it is important that you create an environment where your athletes feel they can be open and honest with you when needed. As North Carolina men's basketball coach Roy Williams says, "I bring the kids in and we close the door. I say, 'When I close that door you can say anything you want to say from, Coach, you're not playing me enough, to You're a bad coach, to I'm fine, everything's perfect.' I want them to understand that when we come in here and close the door, they can say anything. And then, before they leave, I will either agree with them or explain to them why I don't agree with them and they just have to understand that I'm being truthful." Credible coaches make a real effort to create an environment where coaches and athletes work together and communicate well with each other to accomplish goals.

As a coach, you must remember that communicating with you can be a very intimidating and vulnerable situation for your athletes. It takes a conscious effort on your part to put them at ease and allow them to trust that they can speak with you when needed. Making it known that you have an open door policy is a good step, but the key is that you truly must have an open door policy. Many coaches say they want their athletes to feel that they can stop by and talk. Unfortunately, some coaches aren't willing to put in the effort to make sure their athletes feel comfortable enough to speak to them.

One college basketball coach says that he doesn't have time to worry about whether his players feel like they can come and talk to him about various issues. He says, "That's what my assistants are for anyway." The problem with this mentality is that by not spending the time to nurture trusting relationships with his players, this coach undermines his ultimate goal—which is to win. His athletes don't really enjoy playing for him and he will have a difficult time reaching his personal goals if he is not willing to create an environment of open and honest communication.

How about your situation? Do your athletes ever "hang around" your office before or after practice? Do all players including those who don't play very much just stop by to say hello or talk to you about issues other than their sport? Do you have to encourage your athletes to leave and go home at night, or do they spend as little time as possible in and around your office? Your answers to these questions may influence you to reconsider your approach to having open two-way communication on your team.

Conflict and Confrontation

Because sport is such a competitive environment, conflict and confrontation are bound to occur. As a coach, you are faced with potential conflict every day. You are going to have athletes who show up late for practice at times. They will not all be able to leave other aspects of their lives behind and give you everything they have every day. Athletes are going to break team rules. They will make mistakes in practice. You also will have conflicts with members of your coaching staff. And for various reasons, you will have to confront the other people involved in the day-to-day operations of your program such as the training staff, office personnel, managers, and custodial staff. How you handle conflict and confrontation will go a long way in determining how credible you are in the eyes of your athletes and the others involved in your program.

There are several strategies to effectively handling conflict and confrontation. When you are faced with a possible confrontation, it is crucial to remember to approach the situation and the person with respect. Many coaches see confrontation as an opportunity to "set an example" for others to witness.

An example of a coach mishandling conflict and confrontation occurred a few years ago on a high school football team. While consulting with this team, Greg was approached by several assistant coaches on the staff. They indicated that the head coach seemed to view confrontation as a means for "putting people in their place," and making sure everyone knew who was in charge. Whenever faced with a situation, this coach seemed to confront the other person in a location where others could hear and see the interaction. He clearly wanted to make an example of the person. This would occur with members of the coaching staff, athletes, and support staff as well. No one was exempt from being embarrassed. Needless to say this coach created an environment where all people involved were intimidated by him and did whatever they had to do to escape his wrath. Consequently, the morale was very low and performance was nowhere near the potential this team was capable of achieving. To this coach's credit, when confronted about this situation, he made a real effort to change. Initially, he was not aware that he operated in this manner. No one ever told him how his actions affected the environment around him. When he asked his assistant coaches for specific examples, he listened, apologized, and made a commitment to change. While he has not completely changed his ways, he has made tremendous progress. As a result, his coaches, athletes, and support staff enjoy being around him more and look forward to coming to the office and participating in practices more than ever before. Credible coaches view confrontation as a way to get everyone on the same page rather than a competition they have to win or a means to make examples of people.

Be Happy Your Athletes Ask "Why?"

Another time when conflict often occurs between coaches and athletes is when athletes ask questions regarding why they are doing something. No doubt, there are various ways athletes can question their coach. Sometimes athletes question a coach with a sarcastic tone or seem to question almost everything that is done. These athletes need to be confronted in private and told how their behavior is unacceptable. However, there will be many times your athletes will not understand why they are doing something and will ask about it in a respectful way. In this case it is important to explain why you are having them shoot the ball a particular way or running a certain offense against a particular defense.

Jerry Welsh, a scout for the NBA's Milwaukee Bucks and a former four-time NCAA Division III Basketball Coach of the Year, says that it is important to explain why you are doing something from the very beginning. For example, when you demonstrate the way you want a particular skill to be executed or you have your athletes run certain plays, you should explain why these things are important. He feels explaining to your athletes why you have them do something is an important aspect of good teaching. The "why" should always be given right along with the "what."

If you don't explain the "why" during your teaching, you should expect some questions. If you become defensive when athletes ask you why, they are going to be much less inquisitive and willing to learn. They will also view you as being insecure in your position and will lose some measure of respect for you. It is important to realize that athletes of today want to know why. This doesn't mean that they are questioning your authority. They are taught to question things today. We have found that credible coaches encourage their athletes to question things and view it as a positive sign they are eager to learn and perform.

"Some coaches get upset when their players ask them 'Why?' I think a coach should get excited because it shows the kid is interested."

Mike Candrea, University of Arizona Softball

"I think the athlete of today is much more savvy. They want to know why they are doing what they are doing and I think that is good. I try very hard to let my players understand why we are doing certain things."

Jerry Yeagley, Indiana University Men's Soccer

Take a Proactive Approach

In addition to treating other people with respect, credible coaches are proactive in resolving conflicts with their athletes and others involved with the program. They seek out people and initiate communication rather than waiting for others to always take the initial step. Credible coaches tend to be in tune with what is happening with the people around them so they are able to attend to potential problems before they become explosive.

"People talk to you in different ways—through facial expressions, moods, mannerisms, body language, the tone in their voice, the look in their eyes. As a coach, I must be able to read my players, to recognize those different things and then take appropriate action. This aspect of leadership is fascinating to me."

Mike Krzyzewski, Duke University Men's Basketball

While it is important to be proactive in your confrontation, it is also important to use proper timing. You must know your athletes, fellow coaches, and support staff and get a feel for when you should confront them. Joe Torre, the manager of the New York Yankees, has some great insights into the art of one-to-one communication in his book *Ground Rules for Winners*. Torre says, "Timing is everything. Once you've identified the best kind of communication needed, you've got to determine the best time to have that talk. Your decision must be based on your gut sense of when he or she is receptive. You might have exactly the right thing to say, but if the door is closed it won't make a bit of difference."

You have to know when to nudge the door open with helpful, directive comments. The people you are confronting have to be in a situation where they are receptive to your comments. This is not to say that people will always agree with what you have to say or that they will not be resistant or even hostile at times. But, taking the time to get to know the people around you, being in tune with their particular situations and treating them with respect will enhance your chances of effectively handling a confrontation.

It's Not Just What You Say

One aspect of feedback that is often overlooked is the significance of a coach's nonverbal messages. It has been reported that up to 90% of the meaning of a message is translated by our nonverbal communication. If that is true, it only makes sense for you to be aware of your nonverbal messages and seek to make sure they are effective. Many coaches are not aware of the messages they send. Or they think they are using nonverbal messages effectively when in reality they are not.

Lou Holtz, the head football coach at the University of South Carolina, tells an enlightening story regarding his lack of awareness concerning his interactions with players. They were getting ready to send out a recruiting video to prospective football student-athletes when he was the head coach at Notre Dame. His recruiting coordinator asked him to view it before they sent the tape to the prospects. After viewing the film, Coach Holtz told his recruiting coordinator that it was a great video and he would be excited about coming to Notre Dame if he was a prospective student-athlete. But, he said, it would have been nice if you could have put a few shots of me having positive interactions with my players. Coach Holtz goes on to say that the recruiting coordinator looked him in the eyes and said, "Coach we looked and looked for examples like that, but we couldn't find any." Lou was surprised at this because he prided himself on being positive and sending positive messages. He indicated he learned from that situation and attempts to be more aware of the interactions he has with his players.

A second example concerns another college football coach at a major Division I university who sent conflicting messages to his athletes. He would say one thing, but his nonverbal messages communicated something different. As a result of working with a peak performance consultant, this coach agreed to be filmed during a game and also wore a microphone. The camera was focused on him during the entire game. Later in the week, he sat down with the consultant to view the film and chart his behavior. He was amazed to see how many times his nonverbal messages were not consistent with what he was saying. For instance, one time he yelled to one of his lineman, "That's ok, that was good effort. C'mon, you'll get it next time." Immediately after that comment, he turned away from the kid and threw his cap on the ground and put his hands on his hips. What message do you think the athlete received from that scenario—his coach appreciated his effort or his coach was disappointed in him? He most likely got the message that his coach was not really happy with his effort. The verbal message was not genuine.

To maintain credibility with your athletes, you have to work hard at making your nonverbal messages align with your verbal messages. If you verbalize one thing and your body language says something different, your athletes will pick up on your nonverbal as the real message you are sending. Sending mixed messages only confuses your athletes and inhibits their ability to perform at a high level. You might consider asking someone to videotape you during a practice or game. Ideally, you should be able to hear what you say and see what you do on the video. Watch the video and chart your comments and behavior. There is something enlightening about watching yourself on tape. After all, athletes are videotaped and their performance is evaluated all of the time. Shouldn't their coaches be aware of how they are doing their jobs?

A second area where credible coaches seem to excel is providing approval with nonverbal messages. It is amazing how much of an impact a simple gesture like patting an athlete on the shoulder or back can make. You don't really have to speak at all to send an athlete the very powerful message that you appreciate his or her effort or performance.

Communication Before, During, and After Competition

The following are a few reminders concerning the way you communicate with your athletes in and around competition. As you already know, what you say and how you say it during these times can have a major impact on the performance of your athletes.

Before Competition

1. Everyone prepares differently for competition. It is a mistake to assume that all of your athletes prepare the same way or that they prepare the way you did when you were an athlete. You have to make the effort to find out how they prepare. The team can be broken into subunits and different coaches can be responsible for each subunit if you have large numbers on your teams.

2. Use reminders to focus on the process of playing well. Avoid emphasizing the importance of winning. The process of playing well is much more under your athletes' control and they will be much less stressed or anxious if they have specific aspects of the game to focus on. We recommend coming up with three to five keys to have your players focus on that are within their control.

3. Do not provide them with an out. For example avoid saying things like "I know you are tired" or "We are banged up." Saying these things only provides your athletes with built-in excuses if things aren't going well or they are tired.

During Competition

1. Communications should be simple and to the point. Provide them with simple focus cues. For example, a track coach might tell a sprinter to "stay low" in the start of a race. Or a baseball or softball coach might remind a hitter to "focus on the pitcher's release point."

2. Be aware of your body language. Remember that your athletes will not hear what you say if your body is saying something different. You can create a fear of failure in some athletes just by a facial expression or throwing up your hands in disgust.

3. When in doubt about whether you should say something to an athlete, avoid saying anything. In crucial situations, our ability to pay attention to many things at once becomes diminished. If you sense that an athlete is already overwhelmed, it might be best to leave him or her alone. When you do give instructions during a timeout, for instance, you should ask athletes to repeat what you said or ask them to tell you what they are supposed to do on the next play or in the next few moments. Many times they will look right at you and not hear a word you say. At least when they have to repeat it, you will know they heard what you wanted them to hear. It is also a good idea to ask the substitutes what you said or what the ones playing are supposed to do on the next play. This will help your substitutes pay attention and be in tune with what is happening.

4. Avoid using the word "don't" when giving instructions. When you say things like, "Don't fumble the ball," "Don't turn the ball over," or "Don't swing so hard," you are actually setting your athletes up to do exactly what you are hoping they will not do. By saying these things, you actually focus them on what they are not supposed to do. You should always state instructions in a way that tells the athlete what you do want them to do. For example, "Hold on to the ball," "Focus on a fluid and relaxed swing."

5. Following a mistake, try to ask your athlete questions like "What did you see out there?" or "What do you think you could have done differently in that situation?" Many times a coach's first reaction is to yell or scream things like "Why did you do that?" or "I can't believe you just did that!" Statements like these only put your athletes on the defensive and serve little purpose in correcting the mistake. However, if you ask them what they saw, they will be less likely to tune you out and more likely to remember the proper response in the next situation. If their answer is wrong, you can point out that you saw something different and let them know what you want them to do in the future.

After Competition

1. Give yourself and your athletes some time to cool down after a frustrating loss. A well respected coach says that venting your anger is selfish. You do it to make yourself feel better. While most of the time this coach is able to follow this suggestion, he recalled a time when he blasted his team after a game they should have won against Harvard. He let his anger get the best of him and said some things he later regretted. After having some time to think about his actions, he apologized to the team. He realized he was being selfish in his angry outburst.

2. When addressing a frustrating loss, be sure to point out a few positive aspects of the performance first. Address the areas that need improvement and then design specific strategies to enhance those areas the next time you practice.

LISTEN UP COACHES!

Coaches spend the bulk of their time providing feedback to their athletes. After all, this is how you help people improve. But you must remember that talking is only one half of the communication equation—the other half is listening. One of the biggest differences between credible coaches and coercive coaches is that credible coaches understand the sheer power of listening. For credible coaches, listening is actually more important than talking. When you truly take the time to listen to your athletes, you will discover how to motivate them, build their confidence, show them you care, and help them improve. As Stephen Covey, author of the *7 Habits of Highly Effective People* puts it, "Seek first to understand, then to be understood."

"You have to listen to develop effective, meaningful relationships with people... As a coach, I need to know a lot about them, and a lot about their families, their goals, and their dreams. You can't do that by talking. You do that by listening. What I have learned is, coaching is not all about me going into a locker room and telling them everything I know about basketball. It's a matter of knowing how they think and feel and what they want and what's important in their lives. Listening has allowed me to be a better coach."

Pat Summitt, University of Tennessee Women's Basketball

"The more you listen to a kid, the more they will communicate with you. I work very hard at trying to get to know the kids as much as possible. I think the better I know the kid, the easier it is to motivate them."

Mike Candrea, University of Arizona Softball

Value Your Athletes' Input

Not only do credible coaches listen to their athletes, they also actively solicit their input on decisions that affect the team. By involving their athletes in the decision-making process, coaches show their athletes how much they are open to and respect their opinions. This doesn't mean that you must automatically adopt whatever your athletes want. However, it does mean that you should confer with your athletes, especially your captains and team leaders, to consider their insights before making a decision whenever it is possible and practical to do so.

You can and should ask for your team's input on minor decisions like where the team should eat lunch, what practice time works best for everyone, or which kind of equipment they prefer. These small gestures will only enhance your credibility. Because credible coaches trust their athletes, they often will ask them for their input on major decisions as well. Credible coaches have been known to ask for their athletes' recommendations on such critical issues as how teammates should be disciplined when they break team rules, which recruits would fit in best with the team if offered scholarships, and what plays to run.

For example, Nebraska football coach Tom Osborne developed what he called a Unity Council with his team. The Unity Council was comprised of elected representatives from each position who were in charge of handling discipline issues within the team. When a player broke a team rule, he had to appear before the Unity Council to explain his side of the story. The Unity Council then decided how to handle the situation. Coach Osborne basically enforced the Council's recommendations. Once again, remember that consulting with your athletes doesn't mean you must follow through with their advice. But it does show them their ideas matter and play a significant role in your decision-making process.

Similarly, many coaches will have their current athletes spend a lot of time with their recruits on the weekend recruiting visits. At the end of the weekend, the coach will ask the current athletes about how well the recruit might fit into the program. If the current athletes have serious reservations about the recruit, most credible coaches will reconsider their scholarship offers and look elsewhere.

Finally, when Pat Summitt was the head coach of the Olympic basketball team in 1984 she had a very difficult decision to make in cutting the team from 18 players down to the required number of 12. What did she do? She handed out confidential ballots to each of the 18 players and told them to vote for the 12 they thought most deserved to represent the team. She says, "When the coaching staff totaled up the player votes, the twelve who won matched the list that we, as coaches, had made. Our first choices were the same as those of the players. I took the 12 players they wanted. It pre-empted potential problems. If you want to have a team, you have to involve the team members in the decision-making process."

Questions for Reflection

- Are you able to effectively communicate your knowledge of the sport to your athletes?
- Do you truly listen when your athletes are talking?
- Do you handle conflicts with your athletes and others involved with your program in a respectful manner?
- Do you know how to best communicate with your athletes before, during, and after competition?

Chapter Twelve Key Points

- Great coaching involves great teaching principles.
- Involve your athletes in as many decisions as possible.
- Invest the time to actively listen to your athletes.
- Proactively seek to settle conflicts in a respectful manner.

DR. LEROY WALKER

Former President of the U.S. Olympic Committee

Head Men's Track and Field Coach
1976 U.S. Olympic Team
U.S. Olympic Hall of Fame

On Confidence Building

You have to understand that all athletes are not alike. You can't treat everyone the same in coaching. You have to treat everybody fairly and you have to be consistent. For example, I had one sprinter who had this aura about him. He was a real hard worker and a good little sprinter. I had another guy who was what you might think of in a kid from the inner city. When I was trying to get something across to the two of them, it was two completely different approaches. I could take the first guy and walk with him down the track, with my arm around him and talk in a normal tone of voice and get great results. He would be listening so attentively. If I did the same thing with the second guy, he would be looking up in the stands or somewhere else and would pay no attention to what I was saying. So, I would take him by the jersey and get him to look at me in the eyes and say, "This is what I want. Do you understand what I want?" There was no slapping him around or anything like that, but I had to get his attention to make sure he was listening to me. This was the most effective method for him. There were two different approaches with the same results.

You don't bash athletes when they make an error. As I said before, you get them involved in the solution. If they don't know, you tell them what they did wrong and then you work with them on how to correct it. I think you really have to be able to critique what your athletes are doing one-on-one. I never ever verbally beat up on an athlete in a team meeting. When I had one guy screwing up, I needed to address that with him rather than bringing everyone else into the situation. The others weren't the guilty party in terms of violating a rule or something. Besides, rather than having everyone else have to listen to me, I wanted to get eyeball to eyeball with that guy and let him know what I think about what he has done.

On Communication

When an athlete would finish executing something, I would always say, "Tell me something about the race," or "Or what do you think happened?" I would do this rather than yell or scream at them. This allowed them to figure out much of it on their own. Yelling and screaming is not effective and it really wastes precious teaching time. The essence of coaching is understanding your athletes. You have to listen to them and find out what they felt, how they interpreted their race. Then you can tell them how you interpreted it or saw it through your eyes as the coach.

I also had to be willing to explain to an athlete why he should do something. This is why we were like a family. We had that type of relationship together. I wanted my athletes to be students of the sport or their event and I welcomed their questions about why we did things the way we did.

On Consistency

You can't have two sets of rules—one for your superstars and one for your other athletes. For example, people ask me what were your rules. I only had one rule and that was that you had to come to practice everyday and be on time. The consequence was that if you were late you had to run a mile. In 39 years of coaching, I only had to enforce that rule two times.

Mike Gillespie, Head Baseball Coach, University of Southern California

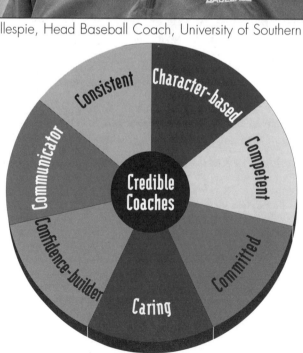

CHAPTER THIRTEEN

Credible Coaches Are CONSISTENT

"To be credible, you must be consistent. Any sign of inconsistency, and you lose credibility instantly."

Pat Summitt, University of Tennessee Women's Basketball

Have you ever worked for someone who wasn't consistent in what he or she did on a daily basis? What is it like to work for someone who doesn't have a consistent philosophy? Do you enjoy working for people who keep you guessing all of the time? Is it difficult to perform at a high level when you have an inconsistent boss who changes his or her mood based on how well things are going? Have you ever worked for someone who promises one thing, but doesn't follow through on what is promised? What happens when you work for someone who has favorites and you aren't one of them? What is it like when you are stuck in someone's "doghouse" because of a past mistake and you can't seem to get out?

If we are honest, none of us enjoy working in an inconsistent, unpredictable environment. And, most of us would agree that it is very difficult to perform at a high level in such a volatile environment. Athletes are no different. They want to know what to expect from their coaches and the environment in which they are expected to perform. They want consistency and have indicated they respect a coach who is able to provide it for them.

We have found that credible coaches tend to be consistent in several areas. They have a consistent philosophy that guides the decisions they make. Credible coaches demonstrate consistency in their exceptional organization skills and attention to detail. Credible coaches are respected for their ability to maintain a consistent upbeat mood and control their emotions regardless of whether their team is winning or losing. Finally, credible coaches are consistent in the way they handle discipline on their teams. We would like to address each of these areas and challenge you to examine your consistency as a coach.

Consistent But Flexible Philosophy

"She definitely has a philosophy that she lives by and she feels strongly about her philosophy of the way things should be done on our team. There are some things that you just know that she will not bend on. But there are other things she is willing to change if she thinks it will help us be successful and not go against her values."

Professional Women's Basketball Player

Credible coaches have a consistent philosophy which they live by to help them with the everyday occurrences on their teams. We already have addressed the importance of coaches having a philosophy statement (see the character-based chapter). Much like assisting you in being a coach of character, having a philosophy statement will help you be more consistent in the way you run your program on a daily basis. By having a consistent philosophy, you will develop a recognized and accepted set of standards on your team or what Mike Candrea, the softball coach at the University of Arizona, calls a "winning environment."

All coaches want to be successful and much of their time is spent trying to come up with the perfect game plan or strategy that will help them succeed. Unfortunately, the importance of developing a winning environment is often overlooked. Developing a winning environment includes factors such as instilling an aggressive attitude, commitment, pride in team and individual performance, building team chemistry, defining the dress code and methods of communication, how practices are organized, and the leadership style of the coach.

"Our job as coaches is to create the proper environment so that athletes can reach their potential."

Jerry Yeagley, Indiana University Men's Soccer

Credible Coaches Often Hire Their Own

Because developing and maintaining a winning environment is so important to a program's success, several credible coaches hire their former players as their assistant coaches. Duke men's basketball coach Mike Krzyzewski has had former players Johnny Dawkins, Tommy Amaker, David Henderson, Quin Snyder, Chris Collins, and Steve Wojciechowski serve as assistant coaches. Similarly, Arizona softball Coach Mike Candrea's staff has been comprised of former players Lisa Bernstein-O'Brien, Jody Pruitt, Stacy Iveson, Nancy Evans, Jenny Dalton-Hill, Leah O'Brien, Krista Gomez, and Alison Johnsen-McCutcheon.

By hiring their former players as assistants, these coaches maintain a sense of continuity in their program. They don't have to worry about orienting new staff members to their philosophy and expectations since it was already well ingrained in them when they were athletes. Not surprisingly, these assistant coaches are very attractive candidates when coaching positions come available and many of them eventually go on to lead their own programs.

Creating and Maintaining a Winning Environment

Following are a few general reminders to help you create and maintain a winning environment on your team.

1. Organization and attention to detail are essential. Credible coaches leave nothing to chance and are always prepared for practice and games.

2. The coaching staff should always be "on the same page" regarding everyday occurrences on the team. Meeting times should be consistent from day to day if possible. These meetings should be organized and efficient with respect to time. It is frustrating for assistant coaches to sit through extended, unnecessary meetings. They have many tasks to accomplish and not enough time to do everything. Your meetings will be much more productive if you have an agenda, you follow that agenda, and you stick to the time frame you have allotted.

3. Develop a practice plan and put it in a format that you can use. Type your plan and put it on a single piece of paper or an index card to be referred to during practice.

4. Provide all members of the coaching staff a copy of the final practice schedule (that they hopefully helped create) well before the scheduled practice time. This will allow your assistants to prepare appropriately. If you are an assistant, it is important to review the practice plan before you begin practice each day. You also can help your athletes better prepare for practice if you inform them of the practice schedule ahead of time. You can post it in the locker room or give it to them in advance. This will allow them to mentally prepare for what is to come.

5. Stick with what you plan, particularly in terms of stopping when you say practice will end. One of the quickest ways to lose credibility with athletes is to say that practice will end at a certain time, but you continue beyond that time frame. It is better to say nothing at all than to tell your athletes you will stop at a certain time and not follow through on it. For example, if you tell your athletes that if they work really hard, they will only practice for an hour and a half. Your athletes work hard, but you say we just need to stay a little longer to work on this one skill or play, they will be less likely to believe you the next time. Consequently, because they don't have an idea about practice time, some athletes might hold back in the early phases of practice to make sure they have enough energy for the last phases of practice.

Being Adaptable to Change

All of our discussion thus far has emphasized being consistent with your philosophy on a daily basis. But to be a credible coach you also must be flexible and adaptable. The main area in which flexibility in your philosophy is needed is with the X's and O's of your team. Some coaches make the mistake of finding one way of executing on the field or court and are not willing to change that system to accommodate the unique talents of different personnel.

For example, what happens if you have a very mobile quarterback who runs your option offense very well, but gets injured? Your backup quarterback is not nearly as mobile, but is a better passer. Do you try to make this quarterback run the option offense because "your teams run the option offense" or do you make some adjustments and try to throw the ball more?

One high school basketball coach has made the argument that he always plays man-to-man defense. He has developed a system for this type of defense and uses it every year. He feels it creates a tough defensive mind-set. In his mind, this is a good argument for staying with one way of doing things. However, there will be times when you have athletes who don't have the skills to run a certain type of offense or defense. What if you have five basketball players who lack quickness and/or speed? As hard as they work in practice and as fit as they might become, they are not able to play a man-to-man defense effectively. They simply do not have the physical tools to execute it properly. Do you insist on running that defense because it is your philosophy, or do you make adjustments according to your personnel? This is a time when flexibility might be best to utilize the strengths of your athletes.

There must be a balance between having a system and adapting your system when different people begin playing for you or when injuries occur. Former UCLA basketball coach John Wooden played a high post offense relying on his team's quickness the majority of the time he coached except for the years he had Lou Alcindor and Bill Walton. During those years, the Bruins ran a low post offense to take advantage of the strength they had in that position.

Mike Krzyzewski made adjustments when center Carlos Boozer was injured late in Duke's 2001 national championship season. Because Boozer's strong inside presence was not available, the Blue Devils made adjustments to take advantage of their quickness and speed. In particular, in the final game of the regular season against the University of North Carolina, the plan was to limit the number of touches for Carolina's big man Brendan Haywood. Duke put more pressure on the ball and caused more turnovers, which in turn did limit the number of times Haywood touched the ball. This is another example of a coach being open to change.

Don Shula, the Hall of Fame Miami Dolphins football coach, captures our message regarding the importance of being flexible and making the most out of the personnel you have when he said, "That to me is what coaching is all about. You take the talent you have, analyze it and put in a system that gets the most out of their abilities, rather than force a system. In '72-73, we had the great physical talent with Csonka and the offensive line. Some called it businesslike, even boring. But that approach worked. With Marino, it just wouldn't have made sense."

Managing Your Moods

"The coach I am playing for now isn't very consistent. We never know what to expect from him from one day to the next. One day he can be in a great mood and the next he is in a funk and looking to bite someone's head off. The coach I had before this one was much better at being consistent from day to day. At least we knew what to expect from him."

College Men's Soccer Player

One of a coach's biggest frustrations is the inability of his or her athletes to control their moods and emotions, especially when they are under stress. To have quality practices, you need your athletes to be mentally and emotionally ready to give 100% and not be distracted by anything else that has happened during the day. You want them to leave their excess baggage in the locker room and come in focused on what they need to do to have a great practice.

It is even more important that your athletes control their moods and emotions in competition. You expect them to be able to handle a variety of difficult situations such as overly aggressive opponents, terrible calls by officials, poor playing and weather conditions, and hostile crowds. If your athletes aren't able to maintain their composure and mental toughness in competition, your team's chances of success are severely minimized. Just as coaches want their athletes to be able to manage their moods, stresses, and emotions for the good of the team so, too, do your athletes expect you to manage yours.

There is little doubt that your mood can have a tremendous influence on the practice environment. One story that illustrates the degree to which a coach can affect the practice environment involves a college basketball team. The head coach arrives at practice sometime during stretching. Several athletes on this team indicate that they can tell what type of practice it will be that day based on the way the coach walks in the gym. If he is smiling, they know practice will be upbeat, positive, and productive. If he is mad about something, he tends to be more negative and creates an environment that is not very productive.

If you want to become a credible coach, you must work very hard at displaying a consistent mood regardless of your win-loss record or what is going on in your personal life. We aren't saying that practices following losses because of a lack of effort or execution shouldn't be more intense. We are saying, however, that you must maintain an even keel emotionally whether your team is on a 10 game winning streak or losing streak. As University of Arizona softball coach Mike Candrea says, "You can't let the highs get too high or the lows get too low."

"If I come in to practice on a downer, that's exactly how the players will respond. My job, no matter what has transpired before 3:00, is to come in focused and ready to go. They deserve that. That's what I get paid for. They deserve my best effort and that has to be consistent. If we expect consistency from them, they have to see it from us."

Mary Wise, University of Florida Volleyball

Credible Coaches Keep Hope Alive

Obviously it is easy to be upbeat and create a positive environment when things are going well on and off the playing field. The toughest challenge of coaching is being positive, patient, and optimistic when your team has just lost three in a row, your best player is out for the rest of the season, your prized recruit has committed to your rival school, your children are sick, and your contract is up at the end of the year. It would be very easy to take your frustrations out on your athletes by snapping at them for mistakes, running them extra hard, and throwing in the proverbial towel, but doing so only makes the situation worse. Remember that every coach goes through tough times—even Dean Smith and Mike Krzyzewski. Although now they are Hall of Fame coaches, both Coach Smith and Coach Krzyzewski were almost run out of town early in their careers by skeptical and impatient fans and boosters. Despite their doubters, these two legendary coaches persisted and kept building toward a positive future. Imagine what would have happened if either of them had given up when times were tough.

No matter how bad things seem, you must somehow maintain a sense of optimism. To accomplish this, credible coaches must have incredible reserves of energy deep within themselves. You must dig down deep and keep fighting even though you just received a series of knockout punches. In essence, you must keep hope alive for yourself and your athletes when it would be so much easier to give up and give in. Once your athletes sense you have given up on them, you will lose all credibility and your athletes will very likely give up on themselves.

"When we lose, I've got to put on a new, winning, confident, enthusiastic face."
Tommy Lasorda, Former Los Angeles Dodgers Coach

"Fall down seven times, stand up eight."
Chinese Proverb

If you have a difficult time maintaining a consistent mood from one day to the next, you should attempt to find a way to make the transition from dealing with the everyday stressors of your life to becoming a coach. Find something that you can do before each practice that will help you make this transition. Jeff Meyer, former head basketball coach at Liberty University and now an assistant at Butler University, uses putting on his whistle as his signal that he is now a coach. He is no longer a father, husband, or employee. He is "there" for his athletes. Occasionally, when something stressful has happened that day, he will tell his team about it to illustrate his commitment and ability to put it behind him to focus on practice. This also can help your athletes view you as human and thus relate to the struggles that you face everyday.

Controlling Your Emotions

In addition to being able to manage their moods, credible coaches are also able to control their emotions and stay calm in pressure situations. Once again, this is much easier said than done. As a coach it is only natural to get caught up in the competition emotionally. After all, your pride, reputation, and possibly your income are all riding on the outcome of a game played either by innocent children, inconsistent teenagers, or inconsiderate adults—depending on whether you are coaching at the youth, high school, college, or professional levels. Therefore, it is easy to understand how stressful the coaching profession really is at times. As evidence of this, researchers have had coaches strap on heart monitors before games to record their heart rates throughout the game. These studies have found that coaches experience dangerously high heart rate levels at various points during games. There is no doubt that controlling your emotions during a highly charged game is an extremely challenging task.

If you are unable to adequately control your emotions, you may find yourself doing and saying some hurtful things. All of us, at some time or another, have done or said something in the heat of an emotionally charged moment that we later regretted. Louisville men's basketball coach Rick Pitino says, "My greatest failings as a leader have come when I've lost my temper. When you can't control your emotions you can cause harm, for those kind of eruptions are harmful to the group." Those eruptions are also harmful to your credibility.

Coaches must especially learn to control their emotions after frustrating losses. "You can't let your emotions control your brain," says Arizona softball coach Mike Candrea. After a tough loss, it is very easy for a coach to go into the locker room and let the team have it. Because you are probably frustrated or embarrassed, you may have a tendency to blame the team for the loss, or worse yet, single out individuals. This is a potentially explosive situation because not only are your emotions racing, your athletes' emotions are as well.

Former North Carolina men's basketball coach Dean Smith relates a time early in his career when he let two of his players really have it after a loss. Coach Smith admits he lost control and said some things he probably wouldn't have normally said. Unfortunately his temporary tirade severely damaged his relationship with the players for the rest of the season. Coach Smith said he learned a lot from the experience. After that, he made up his mind that he would give a few general comments after a game, but he wouldn't really evaluate it until the next day with his players–after both of them had an opportunity to cool off and collect themselves. We encourage you to heed Coach Smith's advice and consider waiting until the next day to do a complete evaluation of your team's play, especially after a tough loss.

Can You Show the Face Your Team Needs to See?

To illustrate how important a leader's composure is to the team's success, consider the following example. After a relatively easy pregnancy, Jeff and his wife Kristi had some scary complications with the birth of their first child, Ryan. When Kristi experienced contractions during the latter stages of labor, Ryan's heart rate plummeted to dangerous levels. The special care nurses were quickly called in. Since this was Jeff and Kristi's first pregnancy, they were obviously alarmed and unsure of what was going to happen. Each time the heart rate monitor would sound its piercing alarm, Jeff and Kristi immediately looked to their doctor, Jennifer Hutchison, to gauge her reaction. Despite the stress and seriousness of the situation, Dr. Hutchison remained remarkably composed as she did her job. Her calm demeanor during such a stressful time tremendously eased Jeff and Kristi's fears. Fortunately, the danger soon subsided and Ryan was born happy and healthy to the extreme relief and joy of his parents. Just as Jeff and Kristi turned to Dr. Hutchison to see how she was reacting in a time of potential panic, so too will your players look to you and your response when they are under stress.

Mark Jackson of the New York Knicks respects the way his coach, Jeff Van Gundy, handles pressure situations. "He's a player's coach, but the best thing about him is his preparation. He's as good as it gets. When you're down or things are going badly, the coach can panic, which leads to panic by everybody. But, Jeff doesn't panic. He just pushes the right buttons. He challenges us, and we in turn have to challenge ourselves." It is clear from this description that Mark sees the value of his coach being calm when the pressure is on or when things aren't going well. By being consistently calm, Coach Van Gundy's players will more likely be calm.

"Athletes want coaches who are consistent. They don't want to see a different person on the bench during the match in critical situations they haven't seen in practice."

Terry Pettit, Former University of Nebraska Volleyball Coach

How would your athletes describe you and your emotions in pressure situations? Would they say that you are calm and under control? Or would they say that your reaction to these types of situations causes them to be more nervous or panic? Athletes want a coach who can consistently control his or her emotions when things start going bad or the competition is close.

Credible coaches find a way to maintain their confidence, composure, and concentration despite the frenzy and chaos of the situation. Coach Krzyzewski says it best when he says, "A leader has to show the face his team needs to see." No matter what you feel inside, you must be able to keep your emotions in check, and show your athletes the attitude and posture that is the best for them, not yourself. If they are feeling uncertain, you must show them confidence. If they are feeling down, you must show them enthusiasm. If they are feeling hopeless, you must give them hope. If they are feeling overconfident, you must let them know that they are in for a battle. Whatever the case, credible coaches accurately gauge how their athletes are feeling and then arrange themselves according to what their athletes need most.

"I stop and ask myself, 'What do they need from me?' I want to be wise. At times I am hostile and emotional, and in my early years of coaching, I got frustrated and I yelled. And their game went downhill. Now I've learned to control that and neatly focus on how I can help them. It's not about what I feel— it's about what they're feeling."

Pat Summitt, University of Tennessee Women's Basketball

"If you want a team that's in control, and plays with authority, and is assertive, and proactive, and can stick to the game plan, as a coach you've got to be all of that behind the bench. You've got to show composure and confidence. You can't lose your emotions because that's exactly how your team will play."

Tom Renney, Director of Player Personnel, New York Rangers

Consistent Discipline

"Boy, you talk about losing respect for a coach. If the coach isn't consistent and fair with how he handles punishment, he will have no respect from his athletes."

Professional Football Player

In an ideal world, coaches would not need to discipline athletes. No one would break team rules. And everyone would be highly motivated and do what they were supposed to do all of the time. But, the reality is that discipline is needed at times. We have emphasized throughout this book that if you have credibility with your athletes, they will be more likely to do what you ask and willingly follow you. Nowhere is this more apparent than in the area of discipline. If your athletes respect you and enjoy playing for you, you will spend much less time disciplining them and more time preparing them for success.

The Rules Regarding Rules

If you want to be a credible coach who is consistent, here are four rules to keep in mind when you are establishing and enforcing team rules.

Rule #1: Discipline Begins with You

Even the most highly credible coaches must resort to discipline at times. For discipline to be effective, it must begin with you. As Pat Summitt indicates below, everyone including the coach must be accountable for his or her actions. Your athletes need to know that you don't have double standards and that you will follow team rules just as they are expected to do.

"As a leader, you cannot develop discipline if you don't have self-discipline. It starts at the top. You have to demonstrate that no staff member, no employee, no star player is above the rules. I don't ask anything of our players that I haven't asked of myself."

Pat Summitt, University of Tennessee Women's Basketball

"You cannot expect discipline from others if you cannot impose discipline on yourself."

Brian Billick, Baltimore Ravens

Rule # 2: The Fewer the Rules the Better

A second aspect of effective discipline is to limit the number of rules that athletes must follow. Some coaches argue that you need many rules to govern all possible situations that might occur. We would argue that having too many rules creates a negative environment and limits your ability to be a leader. It creates a situation where you are constantly policing minor rules. Credible coaches tend to have a few rules that are strictly enforced. Mike Krzyzewski, Lou Holtz, and Dr. Leroy Walker indicate the simplicity of their system in what they have to say regarding team rules.

"We have only one rule here: Don't do anything that is detrimental to yourself. Because if it is detrimental to you, it'll be detrimental to our program and Duke University."

Mike Krzyzewski, Duke University Men's Basketball

"I ask our players to follow three basic rules. Do what is right. Do your very best. Treat others like you'd like to be treated. Those rules answer the three basic questions we ask of every player, and every player asks of us. The questions are: Can I trust you? Are you committed? Do you care about me? People might think this is corny, but I don't care. This is what I believe."

Lou Holtz, University of South Carolina Football

"I only had one rule for my athletes. They were required to come to practice on time everyday. That rule was really enforced by the upperclassmen not me. I only had athletes come late to practice two times in my 38 years of coaching."

Dr. Leroy Walker, Former President of U.S. Olympic Committee

You also have to be careful not to establish rules that could paint yourself into a corner. After a frustrating loss, a Division I football coach told his players, "You better be here at 7:00 am Sunday morning for practice. Whoever isn't here, I will consider them off the team." Well, the coach's star linebacker showed up over 45 minutes late because his alarm clock didn't go off and another player had car trouble. The coach put himself in a position where he had problems no matter what he decided to do. The coach ended up keeping the players on the team but didn't start them for the next game. However, the team had already lost respect for him because he didn't follow through on his word.

"I think if you have 60,000 little rules, then you're creating a prison. Then you're going to be forced to react to anyone who breaks any of the rules that you've set up. And if you don't enforce them all to what extent the players think you should, you're losing credibility."

Anson Dorrance, University of North Carolina Women's Soccer

Rule #3: Hold Everyone Accountable

A third component of effective discipline is holding everyone accountable. The first time you allow one of your athletes to "get away with something" because he or she is a "star" you will lose some measure of respect with your athletes. Credible coaches are not willing to sacrifice the trust they have built with their team for a win. The discipline doesn't necessarily have to be equal. For example, if you have a rule that forbids alcohol and the consequence for breaking this rule is that a player will lose playing time. This consequence will be effective for someone who plays a great deal, but will have very little meaning to a person who does not play very much. The key to handling discipline is that your athletes perceive it as being equitable. They will respect you much more if you hold everyone accountable."

"I don't play favorites. I offer no special favors to high-salaried stars or players I like, nor do I show personal preferences."

Joe Torre, New York Yankees

Dr. Walker tells the story of how he had an Olympic Gold medalist on his college team. This particular person missed the bus for an away trip. He was able to get a ride from some of his friends to this very important meet. Once he arrived, he asked coach Walker what time he was supposed to run so he could begin to warm-up. Coach Walker told him not to worry about warming up because he wasn't going to run that day. Only the members of the team who rode on the bus would be allowed to compete. This conversation took place within earshot of several of the other members of the team. Without knowing that Coach Walker was within earshot, one of the freshmen asked an upper classman if coach really was not going to let this Olympian compete just because he was late. The upper classman explained that coach was serious and he would not let him run. The freshman promptly replied, "Well I know one thing, you can bet I will never be late." Coach Walker could have used that Olympic runner that day to help the team, but he felt it was important to stick by his word and show everyone on the team that all were held to the same standard.

Rule # 4: No Doghouses

A final component in the consistency of discipline is that you should avoid holding grudges against your athletes. You must avoid putting players in the doghouse. Athletes will respect you more if you can handle any conflicts you might have in an honest and fair way. Then it is important to "move on" and allow athletes to start with a "clean slate." If you don't do this, you will continually be looking for the negative things athletes do.

And, it will be very difficult for them to realize their full potential if they are continually fighting to get out of your doghouse.

"You can't have doghouses as a coach. It is immature and unproductive. You have to deal with a problem and move on."

Kerstin Kimel, Duke University Women's Lacrosse

Questions for Reflection

- Are you willing to make the extra effort to be consistent with your athletes?
- Are you able to come to practice in a consistent mood?
- Are your rules fair?
- Do you hold everyone accountable when they violate team rules?
- Are you organized both on and off the playing field?

Chapter Thirteen Key Points

- Have a consistent philosophy regarding the daily operation of your team.
- Have a flexible philosophy regarding the strategies and techniques you use from year to year.
- Bring a consistent mood to practices and games, regardless of whether your team is winning or losing.
- Be consistent in the way you handle disciplinary actions.
- Be thoroughly prepared for every practice and competition.

MIKE GILLESPIE

Head Baseball Coach
University of Southern California

One National Championship
National Coach of the Year
USA Baseball National Team Coach 2000

On Character

I don't know any other way to do things than to be forthright and truthful with players. I am sometimes truthful to a fault. I try to make players understand that if they ask a question, I am going to be candid about it. Even in recruiting, I don't want to face an issue a few years later where a kid says, "You told me it was going to be this way and it's not that way now." I feel very strongly about the fact that you have to be honest with your athletes. And, hopefully they will respect that.

On Competence

In my case, I find that it is frustrating to have been doing this for as long as I have been doing it and there is still so much to learn. As much time as I have done it, you would think I would know more. It is an ongoing process of learning. There is so much information out there that is available to us and I try to take advantage of that stuff. I go to clinics and I will listen to someone who I think has something to offer that will help me improve.

I am a firm believer that how we perform is how well and often we train, drill, practice for a competitive situation. There are often situations where we didn't do something well and the kids weren't prepared. That is our fault sometimes and I question whether we have taught it well. If that is the case, we will let them know that it was our fault. You do have to admit when you make mistakes or when you don't know the answer right away.

On Commitment

It is very important for the leader to have passion. It doesn't matter what profession you are in. You can't hide it from players when you aren't charged up about what you are doing. I would like for my players to say that I am very committed to them and our program. If I didn't enjoy the challenge of preparing a real good team and the competition of it, I need to get in another business.

I still have a difficult time handling the defeats. I don't think anyone questions how competitive I am.

On Caring

I don't think we are doing our jobs completely if we are only teaching them how to hit the curve ball or throw the curve ball. There is more out there in life than that. I want my players to know that I care about what is going on in their lives away from baseball. I want them to know that it is more than about just keeping them eligible. I think I have a relationship with most all of my players after they are gone and that is important to me.

On Confidence Building

This was a great quality of Rod Dadeaux. He made you feel like you were the best and that you were going to be successful no matter what. I try to instill a sense of confidence in our players because it is necessary for them to be successful. It is difficult to balance helping an athlete to be confident and challenging him to get better. It takes almost a crystal ball mentality to figure out what makes each guy tick. I try to figure that out, but it doesn't always work. If not, I try to learn from that and not make the same mistake with that guy again.

CHAPTER FOURTEEN

LEAVING A LASTING LEGACY AS A LEADER

How Do You Live Your Dash?

"I would like to be remembered by my players as someone who was passionate for the game and had a burning desire to achieve. But who had the well being of the individual players first and someone who deeply cared about each and every player on the team."

Jerry Yeagley, Indiana University Men's Soccer

"I would like to be remembered as a better person by my players than as a better coach."

Rhonda Revelle, University of Nebraska Softball

There is little doubt as to how coaching success is measured in our society. Coaches from youth leagues to the professional level often are hired and fired based primarily on their abilities to win. While winning is important and necessary for many of you to keep your jobs, we have argued throughout this book that ultimate success in coaching is a result of your credibility as a leader. In our work with very successful coaches and athletes, we have found that credibility is the key component that separates the great coaches from the rest of the pack. Credibility is essential because without it your athletes will not believe in you nor willingly follow you. They will not allow you to take them to the next level. And, you will constantly struggle to get them to buy into your system and goals.

While being the key to ultimate success, credibility is also a precarious phenomenon. It takes a great deal of effort to develop, but can be lost very easily. Having read this book, we hope we have convinced you that credibility as a coach depends on your ability and willingness to focus on the relationships you have with your athletes. It is important to "know your stuff" and be innovative in your approach to the strategies and techniques you teach your athletes—hence our devotion of an entire chapter on this topic. But, as Marty Schottenheimer of the San Diego Chargers says, "X's and O's are way overrated. If strategies and techniques were the key difference in success and failure, people would find the one system that works best and everyone would use that system. True success comes from your ability to relate to and motivate the athletes you coach."

Being a credible coach takes a great deal of effort and time. However, we have attempted to demonstrate that building and maintaining credibility through the relationships you have with your athletes will allow all of you to get more from the experience. You both will be more likely to enjoy long productive careers. And, you will be able to forge quality relationships that eventually grow into lifelong friendships.

How Do You Live Your Dash?

As we come to the conclusion of our journey through this book, we invite you to think about the legacy you would like to leave as a coach. When you think about it, your coaching career is relatively short in the whole scheme of life. Whether you are involved for a few years or dedicate much of your life to coaching, the time you have available to impact people is relatively short. To paraphrase Patrick Morley, author of *The Seven Seasons of a Man's Life*, your career is symbolized by the "dash" between your first and last day of coaching (e.g., 1995–2035). It is very short. Therefore, it is imperative that you invest your time wisely and determine what you will do with the short "dash" you have been given. How are you going to coach during those years? What legacy would you like to leave behind after you are gone? What would you want the important people in your life to say about you when celebrating your career at your retirement banquet?

Stephen Covey, author of *The Seven Habits of Highly Effective People*, believes we should "begin with the end in mind" when thinking about how we want to live our lives. We would encourage you to take some time during your busy schedule and ask yourself some very important questions. You might ask yourself: "What is my purpose for coaching?" "Do I want my coaching career to count for something other than the number of wins I accumulate?" "Do I want to make a real difference in the lives of those around me?" "What are the most important things I need to focus on during my coaching career?" If three players stood up at your retirement banquet to talk about you as their coach, what would you want them to say? What would you want three of your colleagues to say about you?

As we discussed in the chapter on caring, people might mention your win-loss record at your banquet, but you will be remembered most for the relationships you have with the people in your life. The people who care about you most will not really care whether your wins outnumbered your losses. They will talk about what kind of person you were and the type of influence you had on them. Take full advantage of the "dash" you have been given and live your life everyday the way you want to be remembered by those who mean the most to you. The reality is that we will all be remembered for something. What will be your legacy?

HOW DO YOU LIVE YOUR DASH?

I heard of a man who stood to speak
At the retirement banquet of a coaching friend.
He referred to the dates of the coach's career
From the beginning... to the end.

He noted the first and last day of the coach's time
And spoke the dates with tears.
But he said what mattered most of all
Was the dash between those years.

For that dash represents all the time
That he spent coaching on earth.
And now only those who loved and played for him
Know what that little line is worth.

For it matters not how much we win;
The trophies... the records... the cash,
What matters most is how we live and love
And how we spend our dash.

So think about this long and hard...
Are there things you'd like to change?
For you never know how much time is left,
That can still be rearranged.

If we could just slow down enough
To consider what's true and real,
And always try to understand
The way our athletes feel.

And be less quick to anger
And show appreciation more
And love the people in our lives
Like we've never loved before.

If we treat our athletes with respect,
And more often wear a smile,
Remembering that this special dash
Might only last awhile.

So, when your coaching career comes to end
With your life's actions to rehash...
Would you be proud of the things your athletes say
About how you spent your dash?

Adapted from The Dash © poem by Linda Ellis,
Linda's Lyrics, www.lindaslyrics.com

Was this Book Credible?

Finally, just as we have encouraged you to assess your credibility as a coach, we invite you to assess the credibility of this book. We welcome any feedback you might have and encourage you to share your thoughts with us by contacting us via e-mail. You can e-mail Jeff at jeff@jeffjanssen.com and Greg at gdale@duke.edu. Please let us know what ideas might have impacted you as well as any of your suggestions for improving future editions of this book.

ABOUT JEFF JANSSEN

As one of the nation's premiere Peak Performance Coaches, Jeff Janssen, M.S. helps coaches and athletes develop the team chemistry, mental toughness, and leadership skills necessary to win championships.

Jeff has been privileged to speak to and consult with many of the nation's top athletic departments including North Carolina, Michigan, Stanford, Texas, Tennessee, Florida, Arizona, Florida State, LSU and dozens of other college and high schools across the nation. His work has contributed to numerous NCAA National Championships and Final Fours.

Janssen is the co-developer and lead instructor in the world-renowned Carolina Leadership Academy, widely considered the top leadership development program in collegiate athletics. The cutting edge Carolina Leadership Academy develops, challenges, and supports University of North Carolina student-athletes, coaches, and staff in their continual quest to become world-class leaders.

In addition to the sports world, Jeff also works with *Fortune 500* companies helping them gain a competitive advantage in the corporate arena. A member of the National Speakers Association and ASTD, Jeff regularly speaks at the FedEx Leadership Institute in Memphis.

What Top Leaders Are Saying About Jeff Janssen

"Because Jeff has worked with so many national championship teams, he knows what it takes to build and maintain a winning program. If you are looking for practical strategies to build your team's mental toughness and team chemistry, I highly recommend you contact Jeff. His presentation to our team made a big impact on our players and coaching staff."

Pat Summitt, Tennessee Women's Basketball Coach

"Jeff has been so influential in helping hundreds of our managers become better leaders. An exciting and effective speaker, Jeff has done a fantastic job with our programs at FedEx."

William J. Logue, Senior Vice President - AGFS, FedEx Express

Jeff offers several dynamic programs for coaches, athletes and businesses including:

The Seven Secrets of Successful Coaches™ *Workshop*
The Team Captain's Leadership Workshop
Mastering The Mental Game of Sport, Business, and Life Workshop
Championship Team Building Workshop

He is also the author of several resources on leadership, team building, and peak performance including:

The Team Captain's Leadership Manual
Championship Team Building
The Peak Performance Playbook
The Mental Makings of Champions
The Psychology of Sensational Hitting
Winning The Mental Game

For more information on Jeff's resources and programs, please visit www.jeffjanssen.com or call 1-888-721-TEAM.

ABOUT GREG DALE

Greg is an Associate Professor and Peak Performance Coach at Duke University. As a professor, he teaches classes in the areas of sport psychology/performance enhancement and sport ethics. As a peak performance coach, Greg helps coaches and athletes reach their full potential by assisting them with the mental aspects of performance. In addition to his work with athletes and coaches at Duke, Greg consults with coaches and athletes in professional football, soccer, baseball, golf, track and field, and tennis.

Greg is a former middle and high school coach in New York City and San Antonio, Texas. He has conducted over one hundred workshops with coaches and athletes from a variety of high schools and colleges across the country and Mexico. He is a certified sport psychology consultant by The

Association for the Advancement of Applied Sport Psychology and is a member of the sport psychology staff for USA Track and Field.

Coach, Athlete and Parent Products by Greg Dale

Books:

101 Teambuilding Activities: Ideas Every Coach Can Use to Enhance Teamwork, Communication and Trust $24.95

Videos for Coaches:

The Coach's Guide to Team Building $39.95
Goal Setting for Success: A Coach's Guide $39.95
Coaching the Perfectionist Athlete $39.95
Building the Athlete's Confidence: A Coach's Guide $39.95
The Coach, Athlete and Parent Triangle: The Coach's Guide $39.95

Videos for Athletes:

Becoming a Champion Athlete: Sports Psychology Series $29.95
Becoming a Champion Athlete: Mastering Pressure Situations $29.95
Becoming a Champion Athlete: Goal Setting for Success $29.95
Becoming a Champion Athlete: Regaining Lost Confidence $29.95

Videos for Parents:

The Coach, Athlete and Parent Triangle: The Parent's Guide $29.95

Visit www.excellenceinperformance.com or call 919-401-9640.

NOTES

Introduction
6   Rick Pitino and Bill Reynolds, *Lead to Succeed (2000)*, p. 80.
7   Marty Schottenheimer in Ray Didinger, *Game Plans for Success* (1995), p. 9.

Chapter 1: What It Takes To Be A Successful Coach
9   Interview with Mary Wise.
10   Interview with Jerry Yeagley.
10   John Wooden and Steve Jamison, *Wooden* (1997), p. 122.
11   Interview with Marty Schottenheimer.
11   Mike Krzyzewski and Donald T. Phillips, *Leading with the Heart* (2000), p. 54.
11   Interview with Mike Candrea.
12   Interview with Jerry Yeagley.

Chapter 2: How To Win Respect By Being A Credible Coach
15   Pat Summitt and Sally Jenkins, *Reach for the Summit* (1998), p. 12.
16   John Wooden and Steve Jamison, *Wooden* (1997), p. 117.
16   Interview with Mike Candrea.
16   Pat Summitt and Sally Jenkins, *Reach for the Summit* (1998), p.
17   Joe Torre and Henry Dreher, *Joe Torre's Ground Rules for Winners* (1999), p. 53.
17   Tom Osborne, *Faith in the Game* (1999), p. 128.
17   John Wooden and Steve Jamison, *Wooden* (1997) p. 114.
18   Interview with Tom Renney.
18   Billy Packer and Roland Lazenby, *Why We Win* (1999), p. 314.
19   Interview with Fred Harvey.
19   Billy Packer and Roland Lazenby, *Why We Win* (1999), p. 207.
19   Interview with Rhonda Revelle.
19   Mike Shanahan and Adam Schefter, *Think Like a Champion* (1999), p. 182.
21   John Wooden and Steve Jamison, *Wooden* (1997), p. 116.

Chapter 3: The Benefits of Becoming A Credible Coach
23   Brian Billick and James A. Peterson, *Competitive Leadership* (2001), p. 56.
28   Gary Barnett and Vahe Gregorian, *High Hopes* (1996), p. 177.
28   Tom Osborne, *Faith in the Game* (1999), p. 142.
28   Billy Packer and Roland Lazenby, *Why We Win* (1999), p. 258.
28   John Wooden and Steve Jamison, *Wooden* (1997), p. 104.

Chapter 4: The Seven Secrets of Successful Coaches
31   Interview with Roy Williams.
32   Interview with Jerry Yeagley.
32   Interview with Marty Schottenheimer.
32   Interview with Pat Summitt.
33   Interview with Mike Candrea
34   Phil Jackson and Charley Rosen, *More Than a Game* (2001), p. 19.
39   James Collins and Jerry Porras, *Built to Last* (1994), p. 43.
39   *Federal Express Managers Training Guide.*

40   Thomas J. Neff and James M. Citrin, *Lessons from the Top* (1999), p. 188.
40   John Maxwell, *The Right to Lead* (2001), p. 71.
40   Interview with Mike Candrea.
42   Mike Krzyzewski, *Five-Point Play* (2002).

Chapter 5: How Your Credibility Evolves and Develops
45   Interview with Mike Candrea.
45   Interview with Terry Pettit.
46   Billy Packer and Roland Lazenby, *Why We Win* (1999), p. 79.
47   Interview with Pat Summitt.
47   Interview with Jerry Yeagley.
47   Rick Pitino and Bill Reynolds, *Lead to Succeed* (2000), p. 196.
48   Mike Krzyzewski and Donald T. Phillips, *Leading with the Heart* (2000), p. 273.
48   Rick Pitino and Bill Reynolds, *Lead to Succeed* (2000), p. 197.
48   Interview with Jerry Yeagley.

Chapter 6: Could You Play For Yourself?
55   Rick Pitino and Bill Reynolds, *Lead to Succeed* (2000), p. 204.
56   Gary Barnett and Vahe Gregorian, *High Hopes* (1996).
57   Debra Benton, *How to Act Like a CEO* (2001), p. 1.
57   Interview with Mary Wise.
57   Interview with Gail Goestenkors.
58   Interview with Rhonda Revelle.
59   Interview with Pat Summitt.
59   Interview with Bill Logue.

Chapter 7: Credible Coaches Are Character-Based
71   H. Norman Schwarzkopf and Peter Petre, *It Doesn't Take a Hero* (1992).
73   Mike Krzyzewski and Donald T. Phillips, *Leading with the Heart* (2000), p. 273.
75   Interview with Fred Harvey.
76   Gary Barnett and Vahe Gregorian, *High Hopes* (1996), p. 129.
76   Interview with Rhonda Revelle.
76   Interview with Tom Renney.
77   Russell Gough, *Character is Everything* (1997).
79   Interview with Terry Pettit.
81   Mike Krzyzewski and Donald T. Phillips, *Leading with the Heart* (2000), p. 40.
82   Interview with Marty Schottenheimer.
83   Interview with Tom Renney.
83   Ken Blanchard and Don Shula, *Everyone's A Coach* (1995), p. 61.
83   Interview with Mike Candrea.
83   Interview with Pat Summitt.
84   Dale Wimbrow, *The Guy in The Glass.*

Chapter 8: Credible Coaches Are Competent
96   Billy Packer and Roland Lazenby, *Why We Win* (1999), p. 261.
96   Interview with Gary Barnett.
97   Interview with Gail Goestenkors.
97   Billy Packer and Roland Lazenby, *Why We Win* (1999), p. 248.
97   Interview with Jerry Yeagley.
97   Interview with Terry Pettit.

98 John Wooden and Steve Jamison, *Wooden* (1997), p. 30.
99 Mike Krzyzewski and Donald T. Phillips, *Leading with the Heart* (2000), p. 152-153.
99 Interview with Mary Wise.
100 Rick Pitino and Bill Reynolds, *Success is a Choice* (1997), p. 240.
100 Kenneth Blanchard and Norman Vincent Peale, *The Power of Ethical Management* (1988), p. 48.
101 Interview with Pat Summitt.

Chapter 9: Credible Coaches Are Committed
105 Pat Riley, *The Winner Within* (1993), p. 71.
106 Interview with Jolene Nagel.
106 Interview with Bob Jenkins.
108 Phil Jackson and Hugh Delehanty, *Sacred Hoops* (1995), p. 98.
109 James Kouzes and Barry Posner, *Encouraging the Heart* (1999), p. 149.
110 Pat Summitt and Sally Jenkins, *Reach for the Summit* (1998), p. 119.
111 Phil Jackson and Hugh Delehanty, *Sacred Hoops* (1995), p. 215.
111 Interview with Roy Williams.
113 Interview with Mike Candrea.

Chapter 10: Credible Coaches Are Caring
119 Mike Shanahan and Adam Schefter, *Think Like a Champion* (1999), p. 182.
120 Interview with Gail Goestenkors.
121 Dean Smith, John Kilgo, and Sally Jenkins, *A Coach's Life* (1999), p. xv.
122 Tom Osborne, *Faith in the Game* (1999), p. 129.
124 Interview with Roy Williams.
124 John Wooden and Steve Jamison, *Wooden* (1997), p. 151.
124 Interview with Tom Renney.
125 Interview with Pat Summitt.
125 Interview with Terry Pettit.
128 Robert Greenleaf, *Servant Leadership* (1977).
128 Tom Osborne, *Faith in the Game* (1999), p. 126.
129 Gary Barnett and Vahe Gregorian, *High Hopes* (1996), p. 21.
129 Rick Pitino and Bill Reynolds, *Lead to Succeed* (2000), p. 50.
129 Interview with Roy Williams.
130 Interview with Gail Goestenkors.
131 Interview with Rhonda Revelle.
131 Mike Krzyzewski and Donald T. Phillips, *Leading with the Heart* (2000), p. 26.
132 Pat Summitt and Sally Jenkins, *Reach for the Summit* (1998), p. 47.
133 Interview with Fred Harvey.
133 Dean Smith, John Kilgo, and Sally Jenkins, *A Coach's Life* (1999), p. 48.

Chapter 11: Credible Coaches Are Confidence-Builders
137 Interview with Marty Schottenheimer.
139 Interview with Mike Candrea.
139 Interview with Pat Summitt.
140 Interview with Mike Candrea.
140 Mike Krzyzewski and Donald T. Phillips, *Leading with the Heart* (2000), p. xi.
142 Interview with Mary Wise.
144 Interview with Fred Harvey.

144 John C. Maxwell and Jim Dornan, *Becoming a Person of Influence* (1997), p. 52.
145 Chamique Holdsclaw and Jennifer Frey, *Chamique* (2000), p. 68
145 Tom Osborne, *Faith in the Game* (1999), p. 92.
146 Interview with Mary Wise.
146 Mike Shanahan and Adam Schefter, *Think Like a Champion* (1999), p. 160.
147 Interview with Jody Adams.
147 Rick Pitino and Bill Reynolds, *Success is a Choice* (1997), p. 1.
148 Interview with Mary Wise.
148 Interview with Fred Harvey.
148 Rick Pitino and Bill Reynolds, *Lead to Succeed* (2000), p. 40.
149 Mike Krzyzewski and Donald T. Phillips, *Leading with the Heart* (2000), p. 35.
150 Joe Torre and Henry Dreher, *Joe Torre's Ground Rules for Winners* (1999), p. 81.
150 Interview with Mary Wise.
151 Rick Pitino and Bill Reynolds, *Lead to Succeed* (2000), p. 83.
152 Joe Torre and Henry Dreher, *Joe Torre's Ground Rules for Winners* (1999), p. 81.
152 Pat Summitt and Sally Jenkins, *Reach for the Summit* (1998), p. 201.
153 Interview with Jody Adams.
153 Pat Summitt and Sally Jenkins, *Reach for the Summit* (1998), p. 78.
154 Chamique Holdsclaw and Jennifer Frey, *Chamique* (2000), p. 76.
154 Billy Packer and Roland Lazenby, *Why We Win* (1999), p. 187.
155 Interview with Terry Pettit.
155 Interview with Tom Renney.
156 Ralph Sabock, *Coaching: A Realistic Perspective* (1995).
157 Joe Torre and Henry Dreher, *Joe Torre's Ground Rules for Winners* (1999), p. 81.
159 Joe Torre: *Fortune*, April 30, 2001, p. 69.
160 Dean Smith, John Kilgo, and Sally Jenkins, *A Coach's Life* (1999).
160 Billy Packer and Roland Lazenby, *Why We Win* (1999), p. 85.

Chapter 12: Credible Coaches Are Communicators
165 Rick Pitino and Bill Reynolds, *Lead to Succeed* (2000), p. 26.
167 Joe Torre and Henry Dreher, *Joe Torre's Ground Rules for Winners* (1999), p. 81.
167 Interview with Roy Williams.
170 Interview with Mike Candrea.
170 Interview with Jerry Yeagley.
170 Mike Krzyzewski and Donald T. Phillips, *Leading with the Heart* (2000), p. 107.
171 Joe Torre and Henry Dreher, *Joe Torre's Ground Rules for Winners* (1999), p. 82-83.
172 Lou Holtz, *Managing to Win* (1985).
175 Stephen R. Covey, *The Seven Habits of Highly Effective People* (1989).
175 Pat Summitt and Sally Jenkins, *Reach for the Summit* (1998), p. 69.
176 Interview with Mike Candrea.
177 Pat Summitt and Sally Jenkins, *Reach for the Summit* (1998), p. 142.

Chapter 13: Credible Coaches Are Consistent
181 Pat Summitt and Sally Jenkins, *Reach for the Summit* (1998), p. 104.
182 Interview with Mike Candrea.
187 Interview with Mary Wise.
188 Billy Packer and Roland Lazenby, *Why We Win* (1999), p. 185.
189 Rick Pitino and Bill Reynolds, *Lead to Succeed* (2000), p. 204.
189 Interview with Mike Candrea.
190 Interview with Terry Pettit.

191 Mike Krzyzewski and Donald T. Phillips, *Leading with the Heart* (2000), p. 149.

191 Interview with Pat Summitt

191 Interview with Tom Renney.

192 Pat Summitt and Sally Jenkins, *Reach for the Summit* (1998), p. 98.

192 Brian Billick and James A. Peterson, *Competitive Leadership* (2001), p. 53.

193 Interview with Mike Krzyzewski.

193 *Lou Holtz*

193 Interview with Dr. Leroy Walker.

193 Billy Packer and Roland Lazenby, *Why We Win* (1999), p. 93.

194 Joe Torre and Henry Dreher, *Joe Torre's Ground Rules for Winners* (1999), p. 38.

195 Interview with Kerstin Kimel.

Chapter 14: Leaving a Lasting Legacy As A Leader

199 Interview with Jerry Yeagley.

199 Interview with Rhonda Revelle.

200 Interview with Marty Schottenheimer.

200 Patrick Morley, *The Seven Seasons of a Man's Life* (1995).

200 Stephen R. Covey, *The Seven Habits of Highly Effective People* (1989).

INDEX

Photo credits
Dr. Leroy Walker
Robert Lawson

Mike Gillespie
Photo by Heston Quan

Mike Krzyzewski
Photo by Duke University
Photography

Kerstin Kimel
Photo by Duke University
Photography

Mike Pressler
Photo by Duke University
Photography

Gail Goestenkors
Photo by Duke University
Photography

Pat Summitt
Photo by Lady Vols Media
Relations

Marty Schottenheimer
Photo by Washington
Redskins

Roy Williams
Photo by Jeff
Jacobsen/KUAC

Jerry Yeagley
Photo by Indiana University
Sports Information

Mary Wise
Photo by University of
Florida Sports Information

Mike Candrea
Photo by University of
Arizona Sports Information

Fred Harvey
Photo by University of
Arizona Sports Information

The Seven Secrets of
SUCCESSFUL
COACHES

How to Unlock and Unleash Your Team's Full Potential

Jeff Janssen & Greg Dale

To order additional copies of the book:

Call toll free 1-888-721-TEAM or (919) 401-9640

Visit: www.jeffjanssen.com

Or mail your check, money order, or credit card info to:

Janssen Peak Performance, Inc.   or   Greg Dale
102 Horne Creek Court   11 Chimney Top Court
Cary, NC 27519   Durham, NC 27705

Name_____

School/Team_____

Sport_____

Address_____

City, State, Zip_____

Country_____

Phone_____

E-mail_____

Credit Card_____ Exp._____